THE IMPERIAL
AIRWAYS FLEET

THE IMPERIAL AIRWAYS FLEET

JOHN STROUD

TEMPUS

For Angela and in loving memory of my beloved Patricia.

First published 2005

Tempus Publishing Limited
The Mill, Brimscombe Port,
Stroud, Gloucestershire, GL5 2QG
www.tempus-publishing.com

British Library Cataloguing in Publication Data.
A catalogue record for this book is available from the British Library.

ISBN 0 7524 2997 3

Typesetting and origination by Tempus Publishing Limited
Printed in Great Britain

Contents

Introduction   7

1. Aircraft Transport & Travel   9

2. Handley Page Transport   19

3. S. Instone & Co. and Instone Air Line   25

4. Daimler Airway   31

5. British Marine Air Navigation   35

6. Imperial Airways   37

7. The Fleets   47

8. The Aircraft   61

Bibliography   147

Appendix   149

Index of Aircraft   159

Introduction

The Imperial Airways Fleet describes in detail the main British airline fleets from 1919 to 1940, giving details of the aircraft history, layout, identity and fate. Much of this information has been published but to find it means going to numerous sources and this book is the first to collect it into one volume.

The pioneers of the early days have unfortunately all left us, but I was lucky to know several of them and count some, including R.H. McIntosh (All-weather Mac), as my friends. I am also old enough to have seen something of the early days. I first visited Croydon Airport, then on the Plough Lane site, in 1922 at the earliest or 1924 at the latest. I was then three or four years old but remember seeing two single-engine biplanes, one red and one blue, which means that they were de Havilland D.H.34s of Daimler Airway and Instone Air Line.

At that time I lived at Streatham Common and sometimes saw the Daimler D.H.34 with its lights on returning from Manchester to Croydon. I must have seen Handley Page O/400s but do not remember them, but I do remember seeing the last Handley Page W.8b flying over St Albans.

From Imperial Airways' time, of course, I saw Armstrong Whitworth Argosies and in the early 1930s I saw all of the H.P.42s and H.P.45s on their test flights from Radlett. I joined Imperial Airways in 1933 but had to wait until 1936 before I flew in any of the fleets. First it was the de Havilland D.H.86 *Demeter* and Short L.17 *Syrinx* but *Heracles*, *Horatius* and *Hanno* followed and then came *Ensign* and the Albatross.

My work took me to Rochester and I saw most of the Short Empire flying-boats being built and flew in *Courtier* on its delivery flight to Southampton.

John Stroud
Nairn
2004

one

Aircraft Transport & Travel

On 5 October 1916, in the middle of the First World War, George Holt Thomas founded the first British airline, with a capital of £50,000. The objects of the company were 'establishing and maintaining lines...and to enter into contracts for the carriage of mails, passengers, goods and cattle...'

Aircraft Transport & Travel was a subsidiary of George Holt Thomas's Aircraft Manufacturing Company (Airco, formerly Air-Co) where his designer was Captain Geoffrey de Havilland and it was therefore natural that AT&T's aircraft were mostly of de Havilland design. Civil flying was not allowed in the United Kingdom until 1 May 1919, but was allowed between London and Paris from 13 to 20 July 1919 in connection with the Peace Conference and regular international commercial air services were allowed from that August. As early as 15 November 1918 Holt Thomas announced that arrangements were being made for AT&T to operate London–Paris services.

However, Holt Thomas did not have to wait for civil flying to begin. In February 1919 an air parcel service began between Folkestone (Hawkinge) and Ghent to carry food and other items for areas of Belgium suffering acute shortages. This operation was undertaken by AT&T at the request of the Belgian government and operated by Royal Air Force D.H.9's flown by RAF pilots. AT&T's name was carried on stickers on the fuselages. Aircraft known to have worked the service included D628, D1197, D1206, D1213, D1214, D1217 and H4275.

In March 1919, the Royal Air Force began an air mail service between Hawkinge and Cologne for communication with the Army of Occupation and, on 15 August, Aircraft Transport & Travel took over the operation on behalf of the government, using D.H.9's. From November, six special Napier Lion-powered D.H.9As were used. These were G-EAOF to G-EAOK. The operation ceased in June 1920.

It was also in March 1919 that Sir Woodman Burbidge, managing director of Harrods, flew from Hendon to Brussels for a meeting. This flight was almost certainly made by AT&T and must have been illegal.

1 May 1919 was the first day of civil flying in the British Isles after the war and the first flight under the new regulations was made by AT&T's D.H.9 G-EAAA (probably still bearing RAF Service number C6054). The aircraft left Hendon before dawn carrying newspapers for Bournemouth but because of fog made a forced landing on Portsdown Hill. The pilot, Captain H.J. Saint, and passenger, Captain D. Greig, were both injured.

On 15 July 1919, an AT&T D.H.9. was flown by Ltenant H. 'Jerry' Shaw on a charter from Hendon to Paris with one passenger. In spite of the earlier flight to Brussels, this Paris flight was the first recognised British commercial flight.

The big day was 25 August 1919 when Aircraft Transport & Travel began regular sustained London-Paris services. At 09.05 Lt. E.H. 'Bill' Lawford left Hounslow in the D.H.4A G-EAJC with one passenger and goods. This was almost certainly an aircraft positioning flight. The first scheduled service left Hounslow at 12.40 worked by the D.H.16 K-130 (later G-EACT) flown by Major Cyril Patteson with four passengers. Arrival at Le Bourget was at 15.05. The first service from Paris was flown by Lt J. McMullin in a D.H.9.

A major contribution to air transport, still in existence, was Holt Thomas's invitation to airlines to attend the organisation meeting of the International Air Traffic Association. Airlines represented were DDL (Denmark), DLR (Germany), Det Norske Luftfartrederi, Svenska Lufrtrafik and KLM (Netherlands). Sir Sefton Braucker, managing director of AT&T was chairman at the meeting. His son, John, after a long career with Imperial Airways, was traffic director of IATA after the Second World War.

Because of a railway strike in Britain in September and October 1919, AT&T began carrying mail to Paris and between London and Glasgow and in November AT&T began the first international official air mail services, between London and Paris. In April 1920 AT&T introduced the prototype Airco D.H.18 on London-Paris services. This was the company's first transport aeroplane that was not a conversion of a military aircraft. On 17 May 1920, AT&T began a London-Amsterdam service in conjunction with KLM. The first flight was made by the D.H.16 G-EALU with 'Jerry' Shaw as pilot.

Unfortunately, on 17 December 1920, Aircraft Transport & Travel ceased all operations, the company having become merged with the Birmingham Small Arms Co. (BSA).

The terminal area of the aerodrome on Hounslow Heath. It was from Hounslow that Aircraft Transport & Travel operated the first cross-Channel air services.

In February 1919 Aircraft Transport & Travel began a parcel service between Hawkinge and Ghent with food and other goods for areas of Belgium suffering acute post-war shortages. Royal Air Force D.H.9s and RAF pilots were used. D1197, in the foreground, is believed to be about to make the first flight. An AT&T sticker is to be seen below the cockpits.

Passengers, suitably dressed, about to board an Aircraft Transport & Travel Airco D.H.9B. (KLM)

Aircraft Transport & Travel's Airco D.H.9B *Ancuba*, probably at Brussels.

Hounslow aerodrome in 1919 with, from left to right: D.H.4A G-EAJD, D.H.16 G-EACT and D.H.4A G-EAJC.

Aircraft Transport & Travel's Airco D.H.4A G-EAJC at Hounslow in 1919.

Taking aboard baggage before departure of the first scheduled London–Paris service on 25 August 1919.

The Airco D.H.16 which operated the first London–Paris scheduled service,. This view shows it before Aircraft Transport & Travel's name was applied to the fuselage. It became G-EACT.

A later picture of D.H.16 G-EACT at Hounslow. The pilot is Lt H. 'Jerry' Shaw. (*Flight*)

During the September–October 1919 railway strike Aircraft Transport & Travel used this Airco D.H.10 to carry mail from London to Glasgow. (*Flight*)

The Airco D.H.16 G-EAQS had a Napier Lion engine instead of the other D.H.16s, Rolls-Royce Eagles.

On 17 May 1920 Aircraft Transport & Travel and KLM opened a joint London-Amsterdam service. The first flight was made by D.H.16 G-EALU and Lt H. 'Jerry' Shaw was the pilot.

The first Airco D.H.18. This the first de Havilland-designed type built as a civil transport. It entered service with Aircraft Transport & Travel in April 1920. G-EARI was the last Airco-built aeroplane and the other D.H.18s were built by the newly founded de Havilland Aircraft Company.

two

Handley Page Transport

Handley Page Transport was incorporated on 14 June 1919 by Handley Page the aircraft manufacturer, which had already made a series of flights in Britain that May, dropping newspapers by parachute at various cities. Handley Page had acquired a number of its O/400 bombers and converted some for passenger carriage including the O/7 which first flew on 5 July 1919.

On 25 August 1919, the day that international services began, Handley Page Transport made a London-Paris flight with the O/7 G-EAAF but regular operation of a London-Paris service did not begin until 2 September. The first service was flown by Lt-Col W. Sholta Douglas (later Lord Douglas of Kirtleside and chairman of British European Airways). A thrice-weekly London-Brussels passenger and goods service was begun on 23 September with O/400s.

On 11 October, 1919 Handley Page Transport introduced lunch baskets on its services. These cost 3 shillings (15 pence) and were the first airline meals apart from those served on the pre-war Delag Zeppelins.

The first newly designed Handley Page airliner, the W.8, flew on 4 December and was exhibited at the sixth Exposition Internationale de Locomotion Aérienne in Paris from 15 December. This type led to a series of two- and three-engine types and it entered service on 21 October 1921.

Handley Page Transport introduced innovative season tickets in January 1920 for the London-Paris route, costing £120 for twelve single flights.

On 6 July 1920, Handley Page Transport began a London-Amsterdam service in conjunction with KLM. It ceased on 30 October through lack of support. A London-Brussels airmail service began on 19 July and on 26 July Handley Page Transport flew an experimental London-Brussels-Amsterdam-Rotterdam operation with British, Belgian and Dutch mail.

The regular London-Paris service ceased on 17 November 1920 also through lack of support but on 4 December, Raymond Vaughan-Fowler flew the airline's D.H.4A G-EAVL over the route with two passengers in 1 hour 48 minutes with the help of a strong tail wind.

Ten days later, Handley Page Transport suffered the first fatal accident to a British scheduled service when the O/400 G-EAMA crashed near Golders Green on a flight from Cricklewood to Paris. On 27 May 1921, Handley Page Transport began working all its services from Croydon instead of Cricklewood. Handley Page W.8bs were introduced on 4 May 1922 and, on 16 May, Sir Sefton Brancker, newly appointed director of Civil Aviation, named two of them in a ceremony at Croydon.

In August 1922, Handley Page Transport created a new record by carrying 260 passengers in a week while a Government subsidy of £15,000 was awarded for the London–Paris route on 1 October 1922.

On 16 August 1923, Handley Page Transport began a thrice-weekly London–Paris–Basle–Zürich service that was subsidised by the British and Swiss governments. The first flight was made by R.H. McIntosh in the O/10 G-EATH.

Imperial Airways was incorporated on 31 March 1924 taking over Handley Page Transport and G-EATH although the aeroplane was never used.

Handley Page's Cricklewood aerodrome beside the London & North Western Railway tracks seen from a Handley Page O/400.

Handley Page Transport's Handley Page O/7 G-EAAF at Buc aerodrome, Paris, on 25 August 1919.

Loading mail on a Handley Page O/400 at Hounslow.

Handley Page Transport's O/400 G-EAAE. Note the airscrews guards.

Handley Page Transport's O/400 G-EAKG leaving for Paris.

Handley Page Transport's O/400 G-EAAG *Penguin* with passengers in the aft cabin and open nose cockpit.

This view of O/400 G-EAKE shows to advantage the layout of the type.

This Bristol Type 62 ten-seater was operated by Handley Page Transport from 1922. It is seen in original configuration. (Bristol Aeroplane Company)

three

S. Instone & Co. and Instone Air Line

On 13 October 1919, the ship owners S. Instone & Co. began a private air service from Cardiff to Paris via Hounslow for the carrying of staff and documents. The aircraft used was the D.H.4 G-EAMU and the pilot was F.L. Barnard. The D.H.4 was converted to enclosed D.H.4A and on 1 February 1920 Instone began using it on a public service from Hounslow to Paris.

On 30 April 1920, Instone's Aerial Transport Department took delivery of the Vickers Vimy Commercial *City of London* and this soon became the best known of all the early transport aeroplanes.

On the last day of February 1921 all British air services ceased due to financial difficulties in the face of subsidised foreign competition. Government subsidies were arranged and Handley Page Transport resumed service on 19 March and Instone on 21 March. With the introduction of subsidies, passenger fares were reduced to the French level of £6 6s single and £12 return.

On 12 December 1921 Instone Air Line was registered with a capital of £50,000. The chairman was Sir Samuel Instone, Alfred and Theodore Instone were directors and S.T.L. Greer was general manager.

On the first day of 1922 Instone Air Line introduced uniforms for pilots and company officers and Instone is believed to have been the first airline to do so. The company also had a very smart royal blue livery for its aircrafts. Instone Air Line began operating de Havilland D.H.34s on the London-Paris route on 2 April 1922 and this type was used when the airline began a London-Brussels service on 8 May.

On 1-2 October Instone began a London-Brussels-Cologne service with the Vimy Commercial but the inaugural flight had to night stop at Brussels because of bad weather. The last Instone service to Paris was flown on 2 October. On 14 May 1923 Instone began non-stop London-Cologne services and in August the Vimy Commercial began working a daily freight service over the route. Instone also made an experimental flight to Prague on 4 August with a Vickers Vulcan but political difficulties prevented regular operations.

Imperial Airways was incorporated on 31 March 1924 and took over the fleet and staff of Instone Air Line.

S. Instone & Co's Airco D.H.4A G–EAMU.

F.L. Barnard in the cockpit of Instone's D.H.4A G–EAMU. (*Flight*)

The Instone D.H.4A G-EAMU taking off from Hounslow. (*Flight*)

One of the best-known airliners of its time was Instone's Vickers Vimy Commercial G-EASI *City of London*.

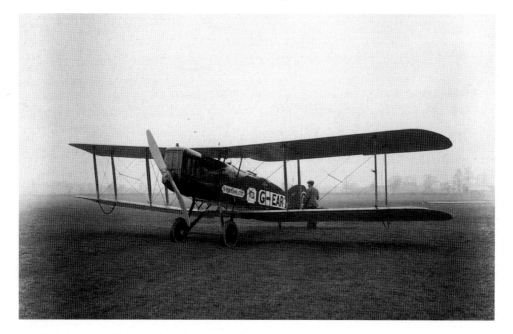

Instone's Bristol Tourer G–EART. (Bristol Aeroplane Co.)

Westland Limousine MkII G–EAJL. Some Limousines were used by Instone after this one had been operated by the short-lived Air Post of Banks during the autumn of 1920.

Instone Air Line's de Havilland D.H.18A *City of Paris.* The style of the fuselage registration is unusual.

Sir Samuel Instone and co-directors, pilots and others of Instone Air Line in front of the D.H.34 *City of Glasgow* at Croydon on 31 March 1924. The standing figures are, from left to right: Capt O.P. Jones, Capt G.A. Hinchliffe, Dennis Handover, Capt P.D. Robins, S. Baxter, Sir Samuel Instone, Theodore Instone, Marcus Davis, Capt G. Powell, C.A. Barnard, Capt. Alfred Instone, Major S.L. Greer, Capt F.L. Barnard and Capt C.F. Wolley Dod. Another D.H.34 and the Vimy Commercial are in the background.

four

Daimler Airway

The Daimler Airway was the aircraft operating section of Daimler Hire Ltd and although the name Daimler Airway appeared on its timetables it did not appear on the aircraft which had the words Daimler Hire Ltd on the rear end of the fuselages.

In October 1922 a revised subsidy scheme was introduced for definite routes and Daimler was awarded £55,000 for a route from Manchester to London and Amsterdam with a connection to Berlin and the airline had to cease operating to Paris, the route on which it began operation on 2 April with the new de Havilland D.H.34 flown by G.R. Hinchliff and carrying newspapers.

Within its first week of operation Daimler lost its only D.H.18. when it collided with a Farman Goliath between Poix and Beauvais. Five occupants of the Goliath and the pilot of the D.H.18 and a cabin boy were killed. Both pilots had been following the road, both on the same side and at the same height.

On 2 June 1922, Daimler Airway's D.H.34 G EBBS broke all records by flying five single trips over the London–Paris route in one day. Then, in September 1922, Daimler made a survey flight over the London–Berlin route with G-EBBS but the service, via Amsterdam, Bremen and Hamburg, was not opened until 30 April 1923.

In October 1922, Daimler began London–Rotterdam and London–Manchester services and on the latter route suffered the first fatal accident to a scheduled British internal air service when G-EBBS crashed near Ivinghoe Beacon in Buckinghamshire. The pilot (L.G. Robinson) and five passengers were killed.

It is worth noting that Daimler aircraft were painted pillar-box red on all surfaces.

Like Instone, Daimler became a constituent of Imperial Airways on 31 March 1924.

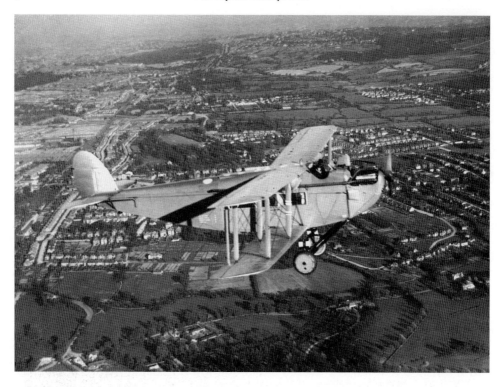

The first de Havilland D.H.34 on a test flight from Stag Lane on 26 March 1922. This aeroplane became Daimler Airway's G-EBBQ.

Daimler Airway's de Havilland D.H.34 G-EBBQ in all-red livery. (*Flight*)

Daimler Airway's de Havilland D.H.34 G-EBBS at Croydon.

five

British Marine Air Navigation

The British Marine Air Navigation Co. was registered on 23 March 1923 with a capital of £15,000 and a promised Government subsidy of £10,000 for services from Southampton to Cherbourg and the Channel Islands. The company was formed by Hubert Scott-Paine of the Supermarine Aviation Works while Shell-Mex-was a shareholder.

The only route ever operated was from Woolston Marine Airport on the river Itchen at Southampton to St Peter Port, Guernsey. This operation began on 25 September 1923 following a trial flight on 14 August from Southampton to Guernsey and Cherbourg. British Marine Air Navigation had a fleet of three Supermarine Sea Eagle single-engine flying-boats. The airline was absorbed by Imperial Airways on 31 March 1924 and the route continued in operation until early 1929.

The hull of Sea Eagle G-EBGR remained as the oldest component of a British transport aeroplane and was presented to John Brancker of BOAC in September 1949. It was wrongly painted as G-EBGS. Stored at Heston, it was deliberately burnt in February 1954.

The Marine airport at Woolston on the river Itchen, Southampton, from where British Marine Air Navigation operated Supermarine Sea Eagles to Guernsey.

The second Supermarine Sea Eagle at Woolston.

six

Imperial Airways

Following the financial problems of the pioneer airlines and the obvious need for subsidies, Imperial Airways was incorporated on 31 March 1924 as the 'chosen instrument of HM Government with the task of developing Britain's commercial air transport on an economic basis'. The new airline was formed out of and took over the fleets and staff of Handley Page Transport, Instone Air Line, Daimler Airway and British Marine Air Navigation. The original capital was £1,000,000 and the company was to receive a Government subsidy of £1,000,000 spread over ten years. Operations were to begin on 1 April 1924 but a pilots' strike over pay and conditions delayed the start of services until 26 April when the de Havilland D.H.34 G-EBCX (Capt H.S. Robertson) operated a Croydon–Le Bourget service.

The original fleet comprised four D.H.34s and the Vickers Vimy Commercial from Instone, three D.H.34s from Daimler, three Handley Page W.8bs from Handley Page Transport and two Supermarine Sea Eagles from British Marine Air Navigation. There were also two un-airworthy aeroplanes which were never used.

Imperial Airways soon adopted a policy of only using multi-engine aircraft (two or three engines) and later went to four-engine aircraft for scheduled services. Most of the airline's fleet was specifically designed for the company and there were never more than eight of one type until the de Havilland D.H.86s of 1934 and the Short Empire flying-boats.

Although Imperial Airways maintained a few European services, the main concentration was on developing the Empire routes. The first segment was opened in January 1927, from Basra to Baghdad and Cairo with a de Havilland D.H.66 Hercules and the entire route from Britain to India was opened in 1929. The England–Central Africa route was inaugurated in 1931 and extended to Cape Town in 1932. The Eastern route was gradually extended, reaching Singapore in December 1933 and the entire route to Australia was opened for mail in December 1934 and passengers in April 1935 with Qantas Empire Airways working the Singapore-Brisbane section. Branch lines from the Eastern route to

Hong Kong and from Khartoum to West Africa were opened in 1935 and 1936 respectively. A service was also started between New York and Bermuda.

In December 1934, HM Government announced the Empire Air Mail Programme to begin in 1937. To cope with the anticipated loads Imperial Airways ordered a large number of Short C class flying-boats and, eventually, flying-boats took over operation of all the trunk routes flying right through from Southampton, whereas before this involved a train journey from Paris to Genoa or Brindisi.

On 1 April 1940 Imperial Airways and the private British Airways Ltd were officially taken over by the British Overseas Airways Corporation (BOAC).

Up to 31 March 1938 (the last date for accurate figures) Imperial Airways had flown 32,036,863 miles and carried 558,927 passengers.

The original Croydon Airport, with Plough Lane running across the top of the picture. The terminal area is in the foreground and aircraft reached the hangars via the level-crossing at the top right. The aeroplane is the Handley Page W.8b Princess Mary. This was Imperial Airway's main base until 1928.

Imperial Airway's de Havilland D.H.34 G-EBBT was one of the four taken over from Instone Air Line.

One of the original Imperial Airways fleet was the Handley Page W.8b *Prince Henry*. It is seen at Plough Lane.

The withdrawal of early Imperial Airways aircraft. They are the Vickers Vulcan G–EBFC, three de Havilland D.H.34s and the Vickers Vimy Commercial. Also seen is the Air Ministry's de Havilland D.H.54 Highclere. The engines from the D.H.34s were used in the Handley Page W.10s.

Imperial Airways de Havilland D.H.66 Hercules G-EBMX at Delhi after making the airline's first flight to India in January 1927. The Hercules was named *City of Delhi* by Lady Irwin in a ceremony at Delhi on 10 January.

Imperial Airways Armstrong Whitworth Argosy G-EBLF leaving Croydon on 30 March 1929 with the first India-bound airmail. (*Flight*)

Imperial Airways Short S.8 Calcutta *City of Alexandria*. (Charles E. Brown)

Croydon Airport in the 1930s. This was the main base of Imperial Airways from 1928.

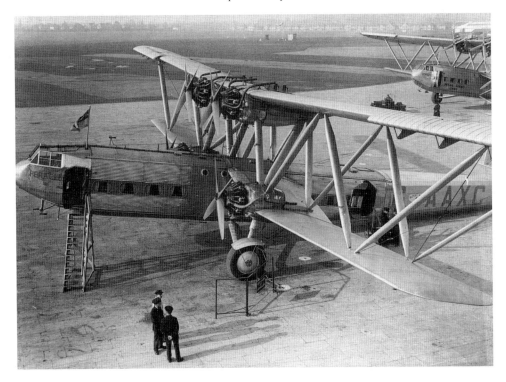

Handley Page H.P.45s *Heracles* and *Horatius* at Croydon. (*The Aeroplane*)

Armstrong Whitworth A.W.XV *Aurora* at Croydon.

Imperial Airways charter fleet in 1933. Left to right they are the Avro Ten G-AASP *Achilles* and Westland Wessex-G-AAGW and G-ACHI.

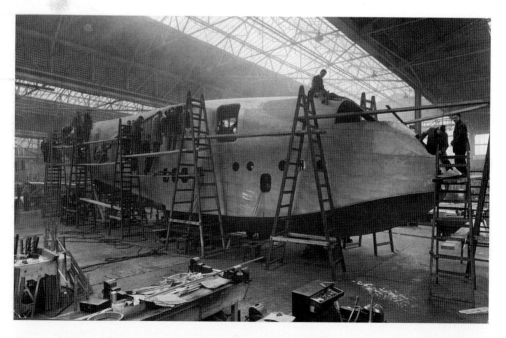

Canopus, the first of the C class Empire flying-boats under construction at Short Bros Seaplane Works beside the Medway at Rochester.

The C class Empire flying-boat *Corinna* alighting on the Medway.

The Short-Mayo Composite Aircraft.

Imperial Airways de Havilland D.H.91 Albatross *Frobisher* and Handley Page H.P.45 *Heracles* at Croydon in 1938 or 1939. Both are flying the Civil Air Ensign. (*Flight*)

Imperial Airways aircraft at Croydon immediately before the Second World War. Included are four Armstrong Whitworth Ensigns, *Ettrick, Eddystone, Elsinore, Elysian,* Short L.17 *Syrinx,* Handley Page H.P.45 *Horatius* and de Havilland D.H.91 *Falcon.* (BOAC)

seven

The Fleets

Note: c/n   = Constructor's number

   C of A = Certificate of Airworthiness

Aircraft Transport & Travel (1916-1920)

Airco D.H.9a (1919-1920)

G-EAOF	ex-E750
G-EAOG	ex-E752
G-EAOH	ex-E753
G-EAOI	ex-E754
G-EAOJ	ex-E756
G-EAOK	ex-E757

These Napier Lion-powered aircraft were used for the carriage of mail to the Army of Occupation and worked between Hawkinge and Cologne. The operation was begun by the RAF, taken over by AT&T on 15 August 1919 with D.H.9s, and the D.H.9As were used from November. The operation ceased in June 1920 and the aircraft returned to the RAF.

Airco D.H.4 (1919-1920)

K-142 C/n G7/63, later G-EAEX

G-EANK	ex-F2670	
G-EANL	ex-F2671	later used to replace lost D.H.4As, sold abroad April 1920.

Airco D.H.4A (1919-1920)

G-EAHF	ex-F2699	C of A	12 August 1919	Crashed at Caterham, 11 December 1919.
G-EAHG	ex-F2694	C of A	12 August 1919	Force landed in English Channel, 29 October 1919.
G-EAJC	ex-F2702	C of A	19 August 1919	Scrapped, November 1920.
G-EAJD	ex-F2704	C of A	25 August 1919	Scrapped, November 1920.

Airco D.H.6 (1919-1921)

K-100   later G-EAAB   C of A   23 July 1919   Sold to Marroni and crashed at
                                                            Croydon, November 1921.

Airco D.H.9 (1919-1920)

G-EAAA   ex-C6054 Reg 30 April 1919   Crashed at Portsdown Hill,
                                                            1 May 1919.

G-EAAD   ex-H9273 Reg 30 April 1919   Sold abroad, September 1919.
G-EALJ   ex-D2884 Reg 26 August 1919   Cancelled, October 1920.
G-EAMX   ex-D5622 Reg 15 September 1919   Sold abroad, April 1920.
G-EAOP   ex-H5579 Reg 20 October 1919   Written off, September 1920.

Airco D.H.9B (1919-1920)

G-EAAC ex-K109 and H9277 C of A   7 May 1919   To de Havilland. Converted to
                                                            D.H.9J.

G-EAGX *Ancuba* ex-H9255   C of A   7 May 1919   Sold abroad. August 1920.
G-EAGY ex-H9258   C of A   12 August 1919   Sold abroad. January 1921.
G-EAOZ   C/n P.3AE   C of A   17 November 1919   To KLM, July 1921, as H-NABF.
G-EAPL   C/n P.33E   C of A   28 November 1919   To KLM, July 1921, as H-NABE.
G-EAPO   C/n P.34E   C of A   6 December 1919   Written off, September 1920.
G-EAPU   C/n P.35E   C of A   29 December 1919   Written off, November 1920.
G-EAQA   C/n P.36E   C of A   12 January 1920   Crashed, January 1921.
G-EAQL   C/n P.38 E   C of A   24 January 1920   Sold to Belgium, July 1921.
G-EAQN   C/n P.37E   C of A   28 February 1920   Crashed at Le Bourget, 9
                                                            November 1920.
G-EAQP   C/n P.39E   C of A   9 February 1920   Sold to F.S. Cotton, 1922.
G-EAVK   C/n P.60E   C of A   20 September 1920   Sold abroad, March 1922.

Airco D.H.10 (1919)

E5557 (D.H.10C prototype) Used on mail service during September-October 1919 railway
    strike.

G-EAJO ex-E5488 C of A 18 August 1919. Crashed March 1920. Owned by Airco. Operated by
    AT&T on mail services during September and October railway strike.

Avro 504K (1919-1920)

G-EAIO   ex-E3359   C of A   22 September 1919   Withdrawn from use, August
                                                            1920.

G-EAIP   ex-E4143   C of A   7 August 1919   Cancelled, August 1919.
G-EAIQ   ex-E-4144   C of A   28 August 1919   Scrapped, November 1920.
G-EAIR   ex-E-4164   C of A   28 November 1919   To Surrey Flying Services,
                                                            September 1921.
G-EAIS   ex-E4170   C of A   1919   Sold abroad, April 1920.

Airco D.H.16 (1919-1920)

K-130	C/n DH16/1 Later G-EACT	C of A	25 May 1919	Crashed, March 1920.
G-EALM	C/n P.1 and 45	C of A	9 September 1919	To de Havilland.
G-EALU	C/n P1 and A/1 named *Arras*	C of A	22 September 1919	To de Havilland.
G-EAPM	C.n P.2 named *Agincourt*	C of A	28 November 1919	To de Havilland.
G-EAPT	C/n P.3 and 44	C of A	8 December 1919	To de Havilland.
G-EAQS +	C/n P.5E	C of A	28 August 1920	
G-EARU +	C/n P.59	C of A	21 May 1920	
G-EASW +	C/n P.6	C of A	30 June 1920	

+ stored at Croydon from December 1920 and scrapped in 1922

Airco D.H.18 (1920)

G-EARI	C/n 1	C of A	22 July 1920.	Crashed at Wallington, 16 August 1920.

Handley Page Transport (1919-1924)
Handley Page O/400 (1919-1921)

D8350 to G-EAAE *Vulture* H.P.16	C of A No.3	1 May 1919	Scrapped, August 1920.
F5414 to G-EAAf H.P.13	C of A No.1	1 May 1919	Rebuilt as 0/7. To USA, May 1920.
F5418 to G-EAAG *Penguin* H.P.18	Cof A No.4	1 May 1919	Crashed, April 1920.
F5417 to G-EAAW *Flamingo* H.P.14	C of A No.2	1 May 1919	Withdrawn from use, April 1920.
G-EAKE ex-J2252 HP.22.	C of A	25 August 1919	Crashed in Sweden, June 1920.
G-EAKF ex-J2249 HP.19	C of A	10 October 1919	Scrapped, October 1920.
G-EAKG ex-J2250 HP.20	C of A	6 September 1919	Scrapped, August 1920.
G-EALX ex-J2251 HP.21	C of A	30 October 1919	Scrapped, April 1921.
G-EALY ex-J2247 HP.24	C of A	17 October 1919	Scrapped, October 1920.
G-EALZ ex-J2243 HP.23	C of A	17 December 1919	Withdrawn from use December 1920.
G-EAMA ex-J2248 HP.25	C of A	7 November 1919	Crashed Cricklewood December 1920.

Handley Page 0/7 (1919-1920)

G-EAAF ex-F5414 HP.13	C of A	14 August 1919	To USA, May 1920.

Handley Page 0/10 (1920-1924)

G-EASX ex-F-308 HP.34	C of A	15 October 1920	To India, April 1921 as G-IAAC.
G-EASY ex-D4614 HP.25	C of A	23 June 1920	To India, April 1921.

G-EATG ex-D4618 HP.37   C of A   23 June 1920   Withdrawn from use, April 1921.
G-EATH ex-D4631 HP.38   C of A   30 June 1920   To Imperial Airways. Broken up,
                                                   June 1925.

G-EATJ ex-F307 HP.39   C of A   25 June 1920   Withdrawn from use, April 1921.
G-EATK ex-J2262 HP.40   C of A   15 July 1920   With Bristol Jupiter engines,
                                                   December 1921. Scrapped,
                                                   August 1922.

G-EATL ex-F312 HP.41   C of A   30 August 1920 Withdrawn from use, April 1921.
G-EATM ex-D4609 HP.42   C of A   30 July 1920   Wrecked at Berck, 30 December
                                                   1921.

G-EATN ex-J2261 HP.43   C of A   13 July 1920   Crashed at Senlis, France,
                                                   14 January 1922.

Handley Page O/11 (1920–1921)

G-EASL ex-C9699 HP.30   C of A   26 March 1920   Crashed, April 1920.
G-EASM ex-C9731 HP.31   C of A   26 March 1920   Withdrawn from use, April 1921.
G-EASN ex-D4611 HP.32   C of A   23 June 1920   Withdrawn from use, April 1921.
G-EASO ex-D5444 HP.33   C of A   15 April 20   Withdrawn from use, April 1921.
                                                   Lion engines.

G-EASZ ex-F310 HP.36   C of A   25 June 1920   To India, April 1921.

Airco D.H.4A (1920-1922)

G-EAVL ex-H5905   C of A   11 November 1920 Crashed, April 1921.
G-EAWH ex-F5764   C of A   18 April 1921   Withdrawn from use, 1922.

Handley Page W.8 (1921–1922)

G-EAPJ *Newcastle* C/n   W.8.1 HP.15   later named *Duchess of York*. Damaged beyond repair,
                                          16 July 1922.

Handley Page W.8b (1922–1924)

G-EBBG *Bombay*   C/n   W-8-2   Later *Princess Mary*   To Imperial Airways.
G-EBBH *Melbourne*   C/n   W-8-3   Later *Prince George*   To Imperial Airways.
G-EBB1 *Prince Henry*   C/n   W-8-4   To Imperial Airways.

De Havilland D.H.18B (1922)

G-EAWX   C/n 6   On loan from Air Ministry   Returned June 1922.

Bristol Type 62 Ten-seater (1922)

G-EAWY   C/n 6124   On loan from Air Ministry   Returned June 1922.

S. Instone and Co and Instone Air Line 1919-1924
Airco D.H.4 and D.H.4A (1919-1922)

G-EAMU ex-H5939   C of A   19 February 1920   Rebuilt as D.H.4A *City of York*.
City of Cardiff   To Imperial Airways.

Bristol 47 Tourer (1920-1921)

G-EART   C/n 58076   C of A   21 April 1919   Withdrawn from use, February 1921.

Vickers Vimy Commercial (1920-1924)

G-EASI *City of London*   C/n 41   C of A   13 May 1920   To Imperial Airways.

B.A.T. F.K.26 (1920-1922)

G-EAPK *City of Newcastle* C/n 32   C of A   4 March 1920   Crashed, 31 July 1922.

Westland Limousine (1920-1923)

G-EARE MkII   C/n W.A.C.4.   C of A   7 October 1920   Scrapped, 19 June 1923.

G-EARF MkII   C/n W.A.C.5.   C of A   21 October 1920   Scrapped, 1923.

G-EAWF MkIII   C/n W.A.C.9.   Leased as reserve   Scrapped, April 1922.

De Havilland D.H.18. (1921-1924)

G-EARO *City of Cardiff*   D.H.18A   C/n 2 and E53   On loan, to RAE, April 1924.

G-EAUF *City of Paris*   D.H.18A   C/n 3 and E54   On loan, crashed, 13 May 1921.

G-EAWO   D.H.18A   C/n 4   To Daimler Airway, 1922

G-EAWW *City of Brussels* D.H.18B   C/n 5   C of A   17 December 1921. On loan, used for ditching test.

G-EAWX   D.H.18B   C/n 6   C of A   23 January 1922. To Handley Page Transport, March 1922.

De Havilland D.H.34 (1922-1924)

G-EBBR *City of Glasgow*   C/n 28   C of A   6 May 1922   To Imperial Airways.

G-EBBT *City of New York*   C/n 30   C of A   28 April 1922   To Imperial Airways, to D.H.34B.

G-EBBV *City of Washington*   C/n 32   C of A   19 July 1922   To Imperial Airways.

G-EBBW *City of Chicago*   C/n 34   C of A   25 August 1923   To Imperial Airways.

Vickers Type 61 Vulcan (1922-1924)

G-EBBL *City of Antwerp*   C/n 1   C of A   23 June 1922   To Imperial Airways.

G-EBDH   C/n 2   C of A   28 August 1922   Returned to Vickers, June 1923.

G-EBEA *City of Brussels*   C/n 3   C of A   28 August 1922   Returned to Vickers, June 1923.

Bristol 75 Ten-seater (1924)

G-EBEV *City of Bristol*   C/n 6145   To Imperial Airways.

Unidentified Instone aircraft names were *City of Ghent*, *City of Liege*, *City of Liverpool*.

Daimler Airway
De Havilland D.H.34 (1922-1924)

G-EBBQ *City of Glasgow*	C/n 27	C of A	6 May 1922	To Imperial Airways,
G-EBBS	C/n 29	C of A	6 May 1922	Crashed near Ivinghoe Beacon, Bucks, 14 September 1923.
G-EBBU	C/n 31	C of A	6 May 1922	Crashed at Berck, 3 November 1922.
G-EBBX	C/n 35	C of A	19 September 1922	To D.H.34B, to Imperial Airways.
G-EBBY	C/n 36	C of A	25 September 1922	To Imperial Airways.
G-EBCX	C/n 40	C of A	30 December 1922	To Imperial Airways.

De Havilland D.H.18A (1922)

G-EAWO   C/n 4   Lost in collision with Farman Goliath F-GEAD between Poix and Beauvais, 7 April 1922.

British Marine Air Navigation (1923-1924)
Supermarine Sea Eagle (1923-1924)

G-EBFK *Sea Eagle*	C/n 1163	Damaged at Alderney, 13 October 1923, and not repaired.
G-EBGR *Sarnia*	C/n 1164	To Imperial Airways.
G-EBGS	C/n 1165	To Imperial Airways.

Imperial Airways (1924-1940)
Handley Page O/10 (1924)

G-EATH   ex-D4631   From Handley Page Transport but never used.

Airco D.H.4A (1924)

G-EAMU   ex-H5939   From Instone Air Line. Used as engine test bed.

De Havilland D.H.34 (1924-1926)

G-EBBR	C/n 28	From Instone Air Line	Crashed in Ostend, 27 May 1924.
G-EBBT	C/n 30	From Instone Air Line	To D.H.34B – dismantled, March 1926.
G-EBBV	C/n 32	From Instone Air Line	Dismantled, March 1926.
G-EBBW	C/n 34	From Instone Air Line	Dismantled, March 1926.
G-EBBX	C/n 35	From Daimler Airway	Dismantled, December 1924.
G-EBBY	C/n 36	From Daimler Airway	Crashed at Purley, 24 December 1924.
G-EBCX	C/n 40	From Daimler Airway	Dismantled, December 1924.

Vickers Vimy Commercial (1924-1926)

G-EASI *City of London*	C/n 41		From Instone Air Line. Scrapped 1924.

Vickers 74 Vulcan (1924-1928)

G-EBFC   C/n 8   Withdrawn from use, December 1925. Dismantled 1927.

G-EBLB   C/n 9   Crashed and burned at Purley, 13 July 1928.

G-EBEK was displayed in Imperial Airways livery at the 1925 Empire Exhibition at Wembley but this was not an Imperial Airways' aircraft, it was owned by the Air Ministry.

Supermarine Sea Eagle (1924–1928)

G-EBGR   C/n 1164   From British Marine Air Navigation. (see note*)

G-EBGS   C/n 1165   From British Marine Air Navigation. Rammed and sunk at St Peter Port, Guernsey, 10 January 1927.

*Withdrawn in 1928. Hull preserved into mid-1950s and then burned, it was wrongly painted as G-EBGS.

De Havilland D.H.50 and D.H.50J (1926–1933)

G-EBFO   C/n 74   C of A   12 November 1923   Converted to D.H.50J

(Jaguar engine)   C of A   14 November 1925   Used on route survey to India and Burma (1924–1925), Cape Town (1925–1926), and as a twin float seaplane to Australia (1926). To West Australian Airways January 1929 as VH-UMC.

G-EBFP   C/n 75   C of A   12 November 1923   To Iraq Petroleum, October 1932, and returned to Imperial Airways, May 1933. Scrapped, 23 October 1928.

G-EBKZ   C/n 133   C of A   11 June 1925   Crashed at Plymouth, 23 October 1928.

Handley Page W.8f Hamilton and W.8g (1924–30)

G-EB1X *City of Washington* C/n W-8-7 C of A   27 June 1924. To W.8g C of A 15 April 1930. Crashed at Neufchatel, France, 30 October 1930.

Bristol 75A (1924)

G-EBEV   C/n 6145   Used for cargo evaluation.

Avro 563 Andover (1925)

G-EBKW   C/n 5097   On loan from Air Council for commercial tests.

Handley Page W.9 Hampstead (1926–1929)

G-EBLE *City of New York*   C of A   20 January 1926   To New Guinea, January 1929, as VH-ULK.

Handley Page W.10 (1926–1933)

G-EBMM *City of Melbourne* C/n W.10-1 C of A   5 March 1926. To National Aviation Day Displays, November 1933.

G-EBMR *City of Pretoria* C/n W.10-2 C of A   9 March 1926. To National Aviation Day Displays, November 1933.

G-EBMS *City of London*   C/n W.10.-3 C of A   9 March 1926. Crashed in English Channel, 21 October 1926.

G-EBMT *City of Ottowa*   C/n W.10-4 C of A   13 March 1926. Crashed in English Channel, 17 June 1929.

Armstrong Whitworth Argosy (1926-1934)

G-EBLF *City of Glasgow*   C/n A.W.154   C of A   29 September 1926   Withdrawn from use, September 1934.

G-EBLO *City of Birmingham* C/.n A.W.155   C of A   30 June 1926   Crashed at Aswan, 16 June 1931.

G-EBOZ *City of Wellington*   C/n A.W.156   C of A   23 April 1927   Renamed *City of Arundel*. Written off, October 1934.

De Havilland D.H.66 Hercules (1926-1935)

G-EBMW *City of Cairo*   C/n 236   C of A   18 December 1936   Crashed in Timor, April 1931.

G-EBMX *City of Delhi*   C/n 237   C of A   23 December 1926   To South African Air Force, November 1934.

G-EBMY *City of Baghdad*   C/n 238   C of A   17 December 1926   Withdrawn from use, 1933.

G-EBMZ *City of Jerusalem*   C/n 239   C of A   21 February 1927   Destroyed by fire at Jask, 6 September 1929.

G-AAJH *City of Teheran*   C/n 240   C of A   7 March 1927   Damaged beyond repair at Gaza, 14 February 1930.

G-EKSH *City of Basra*   C/n 393   C of A   26 October 1929   To South African Air Force, April 1934.

G-AARY *City of Karachi*   C/n 703   C of A   25 January 1930   Withdrawn from use, December 1935.

G-ABCP *City of Jodhpur*   C/n 347 ex-G-AUJR   West Australian Airways. Crashed in Uganda, 23 November 1935.

G-ABMT *City of Cape Town* C/n 346 ex-G-AUJQ   West Australian Airways. To South African Air Force, July 1934.

De Havilland D.H.54 Highclere (1926-1927)

G-EBK1   C/n 151   Air Council owned. Loaned to Imperial Airways for evaluation, 7 November 1926. Destroyed at Croydon when hangar collapsed with weight of snow, 1 February 1927.

Vickers 170 Vanguard (1926-1929)

G-EBCP   C/n 1   C of A   11 March 1926   Loaned by Air Ministry for route trials. Crashed at Shepperton, 16 May 1929.

Supermarine Swan (1927)

G-EBJY   C/n 1173 C of A   30 June 1926   Loaned by Air Ministry. Scrapped 1927.

Short S.8 Calcutta (1928–1939)

G-EBVG *City of Alexandria*	C/n S.712	C of A	25 July 1928	Capsized at Crete, 28 December 1936.
G-EBVH *City of Athens*	C/n S.713	C of A	13 September 1928	Renamed *City of Stonehaven*. Dismantled 1937.
G-AASJ *City of Rome*	C/n S.748	C of A	11 April 1929	Forced down off Spezia, 26 October 1929.
G-AASJ *City of Khartoum*	C/n S.752	C of A	13 January 1930	Crashed off Alexandria, 31 December 1935.
G-AATZ *City of Salonica* [Salonika]	C/n S.754	C of A	3 June 1930	Renamed *City of Swanage*. Scrapped 1939.

Supermarine Southampton II (1929–1930)

G-AASH	RAF S1236	On loan from Air Ministry to replace Calcutta G-AADN. Returned to RAF

Armstrong Whitworth Argosy MkII (1924–1935)

G-AACH *City of Edinburgh*	C/n A.W.362	C of A	19 May 1929	Crashed and burned, Croydon, 22 April 1926.
G-AAC1 *City of Liverpool*	C/n A.W.363	C of A	3 June 1929	Crashed near Dixmude, 28 March 1933.
G-AACJ *City of Manchester*	C/n A.W.364	C of A	6 July 1929	To United Airways, July 1935.
G-AAEJ *City of Coventry*	C/n A.W.400	C of A	21 August 1929	Dismantled 1935.

Westland IV (1929)

G-AAGW	C/n 1867	To Imperial Airways November 1929. Converted to Wessex.

De Havilland D.H.61 Giant Moth (1930)

G-AAEV	C/n 335	C of A	15 May 1929	Ex-Cobham's *Young Britain*, Crashed at Broken Hill, 19 January 1930.

Handley Page H.P.42 Hannibal class (1931–1940)

G-AAGX *Hannibal*	C/n 42/1	C of A	5 June 31	Lost between Jask and Sharjah, 1 March 1940.

G-AAUC *Horsa*   C/n 42/4   C of A   19 September 1931   To BOAC. Wrecked in gale,
                                       Bristol, 19 March 1940.

G-AAUD *Hanno*   C/n 42/3   C of A   30 July 1931   Converted to W.P.45. Wrecked
                                       in gale at Bristol, 19 March 1940

G-AAUE *Hadrian*   C/n 42/2   C of A   10 July 1931   To BOAC.

Handley Page H.P.45 Heracles Class (1931-1940)

G-AAXC *Heracles*   C/n 42/5   C of A   31 August 1931   Wrecked by gale,
                                        Bristol, 19 March 1940.

G-AAXD *Horatius*   C/n 42/6   C of A   13 November 31   Wrecked in forced landing,
                                        Tiverton, 7 November 1939.

G-AAXE *Hengist*   C/n 42/7   C of A   10 December 1931   Converted to H.P.42. Burned at
                                        Karachi, 31 May 1937.

G-AAXF *Helena*   C/n 42/8   C of A   31 December 1931   Converted to H.P.42. Impressed
                                        as AS983.

Short S.17 Kent (Scipio class) (1931-1938)

G-ABFA *Scipio*   C/n S.758   C of A   24 February 1931   Sank at Mirabella,
                                         Crete, 22 August 1936.

G-ABFB *Sylvanus*   C/n S.759   C of A   31 March 1931   Set on fire at Brindisi,
                                         9 November 1935.

G-ABFC *Satyrus*   C/n S.760   C of A   2 May 1931   Scrapped June 1938.

Westland Wessex (1931-1936)

G-AAGW   C/n 1867   C of A   21 October 1929   Converted from Westland IV. To
                                    Air Pilots Training, March 1936.

G-ABEG   C/n 1901   C of A   2 October 1930   Damaged beyond repair in
                                    Northern Rhodesia, 1931.

G-ACHI   C/n 2151   C of A   23 June 1933   To Air Pilots Training, March 1936.

Avro Ten (Type 618) (1931-1940)

G-AASP *Achilles*   C/n 384   C of A   23 April 1931   To BOAC.

G-ABLU *Apollo*   C/n 528   C of A   18 June 1931   Crashed in Belgium,
                                       30 December 1933.

Armstrong Whitworth XV Atlanta (1932-1940)

G-ABP1   C/n A.W.740   C of A   15 August 1932   Damaged and rebuilt as
Atalanta   VT-AEF *Arethusa* of
                                                           Indian Trans-Continental
                                                           Airways

G-ABTG   C/n A.W.785   C of A   12 September 1932   Crashed at Kisumu, 27 July
Amalthea   1938.

G-ABTH   C/n A.W.741   C of A   27 September 1932   Withdrawn from use, June
Andromeda   1939.

G-*ABT1Atalanta*	C/n A.W.742	C of A	2 January 1933	To BOAC.
G-ANTJ *Artemus*	C/n A.W.743	C of A	18 January 1933	To BOAC.
G-ABTK *Athena*	C/n A.W.744	C of A	18 March 1933	Burned out at Delhi, 29 September 1936.
G-ABTL *Astraea*	C/n A.W.784	C of A	4 April 1933	To BOAC.
G-ABTM *Aurora*	C/n A.W.786	C of A	20 April 1933	To Indian Trans-Continental Airways VT-AEG.

Desoutter I (1931-1935)

| G-ABMW Air Taxi No.6 | C/n D.28 | C of A | 6 June 1931. | |

Short L.17 Scylla (1934-1940)

| G-ACJJ *Scylla* | C/n S.768 | C of A | 1 May 1934 | To RAF, March 1940. |
| G-ACJK *Syrinx* | C/n S/769 | C of A | 8 June 1934 | To RAF, March 1940. |

De Havilland D.H. 86 Diana class (1934-1940)

G-ACPL *Delphinus*	C/n2300	C of A	30 January 1934	To BOAC.
G-ACWC *Delia*	C/n2304	C of A	5 March 1935	To BOAC.
G-ACWD *Dorado*	C/n2305	C of A	28 February 1935	To BOAC.
G-ACWE	C/n2306			Transferred to Qantas Empire Airways as VH-UUA *Adelaide*.
G-ADCM *Draco*	C/n2317	C of A	30 March 1935	Crashed at Zwettl, Austria, 22 October 1935.
G-ADCN *Daedalus*	C/n2319	C of A	15 April 1935	Destroyed by fire at Bangkok, 3 December 1938.
G-ADFF *Dione* D.H.86A	C/n2328			To BOAC.
G-ADUE *Dardanus* D.H.86A	C/n2333			To BOAC.
G-ADUF *Dido* D.H.86A	C/n2334	C of A	24 January 1936	To BOAC.
G-ADUG *Danae* D.H.86A	C/n2335	C of A	7 February 1936	To BOAC.
G-ADUH *Dryad* D.H.86A	C/n2336	C of A	7 March 1936	To Aer Lingus as EI-ABT *Sasana*.
G-ADU1 *Denebola* D.H.86A	C/n2337	C of A	18 February 1936	To BOAC.
G-AEAP *Demeter* D.H.86A	C/n2349	C of A	10 August 1936	To BOAC.

Boulton Paul P.71A (1934-1936)

| G-ACOX *Boadicea* | C/n P.71A-1 | C of A | 19 September 1934 | Lost in English Channel, 25 September 1936. |
| G-ACOY *Britomart* | C/n P.71A-2 | C of A | 14 October 1934 | Crashed on landing at Brussels, 25 October 1935. |

Avro 652 (1935-1938)

G-ACRM *Avalon* C/n 698 C of A 1 March 1935 To Air Service Training, July 1938.
G-ACRN *Avatar* C/n 699 C of A 8 March 1935 To Air Service Training, July 1938.
  renamed *Ava*

Vickers 212 Velox (1936)

G-ABKY C/n 1 C of A 30 January 1934 Cargo aircraft. Crashed at Croydon,
10 August 1936.

Vickers 259 Viastra X (1936-1937)

G-ACCC C/n 1 C of A 16 May 1933 Used for radio and icing tests.
Scrapped 1937.

Short S.8/8 Rangoon (1936-1938)

G-AEIM C/n S.757 C of A 26 September 1936 Used for training.
ex-S.1433 Probably scrapped 1938.

Short S.23 C Class Empire flying-boat (1936-1940)

G-ADHL *Canopus* C.n S.795 C of A 20 October 1936 First flew 4 July 1936.
To BOAC.

G-ADHM *Caledonia* C/n S.804 C of A 4 December 1936 Long range
aircraft. To BOAC.

G-ADUT *Centaurus* C/n S.811 Impressed by RAAF September 1939 as
A18-10.

G-ADUU *Cavalier* C/n S.812 C of A 25 November 1936. Sank in Atlantic,
21 January 1939.

G-ADUV *Cambria* C/n S.813 C of A 15 January 1937. Long-range aircraft.
To BOAC.

G-ADUW *Castor* C/n S.814 C of A 23 December 1936. To BOAC.
G-ADUX *Cassiopeia* C/n S.815 C of A 25 January 1937. To BOAC.
G-ADUY *Capella* C/n S.816 C of A 16 February 1937. Wrecked at Batavia,
12 March 1939.

G-ADUZ *Cygnus* C/n S.817 Wrecked at Brindisi, 5 December 1937.
G-ADVA *Capricornus* C/n S.818 Crashed in France, 24 March 1937.
G-ADVB *Corsair* C/n S.819 To BOAC.
G-ADVC *Courtier* C/n S.820 Crashed at Athens, 1 October 1937.
G-ADVD *Challenger* C/n S.821 Crashed at Mozambique, 1 May 1939.
G-ADVE *Centurion* C/n S.822 Capsized at Calcutta, 12 June 1939.
G-AETV *Coriolanus* C/n S.838 To BOAC.
G-AETW *Colpurnia* C/n S.839 Crashed at Habbaniyah, 27 November 1938.
G-AETX *Ceres* C/n S.840 C of A 16 July 1937 To BOAC.
G-AETY *Clio* C/n S.841 C of A 26 July 1937 To BOAC.
G-AETZ *Circe* C/n S.842 C of A 16 August 1937 To BOAC.
G-AEUA *Calypso* C/n S.843 C of A 26 August 1937 To Qantas.

G-AEUB	*Camilla*	C/n S.844	C of A	13 September 1937	To BOAC.
G-AEUC	*Corinna*	C/n S.845	C of A	25 September 1937	To BOAC.
G-AEUD	*Cordelia*	C/n S.846	C of A	9 October 1937	To BOAC.
G-AEUE	*Cameronian*	C/n S.847	C of A	23 October 1937	To BOAC.
G-AEUF	*Corinthian*	C/n S.848	C of A	9 November 1937	To BOAC.
G-AEUG	*Coogee*	C/n S.849	C of A	8 January 1938	To Qantas as VH-ABC.
G-AEUH	*Corio*	C/n S.850	C. of A.	10 February 1938	To Qantas as VH-ABD.
G-AEUI	*Coorong*	C/n S.851	C of A	26 February 1938	To Qantas as VH-ABE.
G-AFBJ	*Carpentaria*	C/n S.876	C of A	25 November 1937	To Qantas as VH-ABA.
G-AFBK	*Coolangatta*	C/n S.877	C of A	18 December 1937	To Qantas as VH-ABB.
G-AFBL	*Cooee*	C/n S.878	C of A	30 March 1938	To Qantas as VH-ABF.

Short S.20/21 Mayo Composite Aircraft (1938-1940)

G-ADHJ *Mercury* S.20

Upper component	C/n S.796	C of A	2 July 1938.	To No.320 (Netherlands) Squadron, R.A.F.

G-ADHK *Maia* S.21

Lower component	C/n S.797	C of A	1 June 1938.	To BOAC.

Short S.30 C class Empire flying-boat (1938-1940)

G-AFCT	*Champion*	C/n S.879	C of A	27 October 1938	To BOAC.
G-AFCU	*Cabot*	C/n S.880	C of A	8 March 1939	To BOAC.
G-AFCV	*Caribou*	C/n S.881	C of A	7 July 1939	To BOAC.
G-AFCW	*Connemara*	C/n S.882	C of A	25 March 1939	Burned out at Hythe, 19 June 1939.
G-AFCX	*Clyde*	C/n S.883	C of A	29 March 1939	To BOAC.
G-AFCZ	*Clare*	C/n S.885	C of A	6 April 1939	To BOAC.
G-AFKZ	*Cathay*	C/n S.1003	C of A	26 February 1940	To BOAC.

★G-AFCY may have been used by Imperial Airways before going to Tasman Empire Airways as ZK-AMC *Awarua* in March 1940.

Armstrong Whitworth 27 Ensign (1938-1940)

G-ADSR	*Ensign*	C/n A.W.1156	C of A 29 June 1938. To BOAC.
G-ADSS	*Egeria*	C/n A.W.1157	Allocated to Indian Trans-Continental Airways as VT-AJE *Ellora* but not delivered. To BOAC
G-ADST	*Elsinore*	C/n A.W.1158.	To BOAC.
G-ADSU	*Eurerpe*	C/n A.W.1159	Allocated to Indian Trans-Continental Airways as VT-AJF *Everest* but not delivered. To BOAC.
G-ADSV	*Explorer*	C/n A.W.1160	To BOAC.
G-ADSW	*Eddystone*	C/n A.W.1161	To BOAC.
G-ADSX	*Ettrick*	C/n A.W.1162	To BOAC.
G-ADSY	*Empyrean*	C/n A.W.1163	To BOAC.

G-ADSZ	*Elysian*	C/n A.W.1164			To BOAC.
G-ADTA	*Euryalus*	C/n A.W.1165			Allocated to Indian Trans-Continental Airways as VT-AJG *Ernakulam* but not delivered. To BOAC.
G-ADTB	*Echo*	C/n A.W.1166			To BOAC.
G-ADTC	*Endymion*	C/n A.W.1167			Allocated to India Trans-Continental Airways as VT-AJH *Etah* but not delivered, To BOAC.

Two other Ensigns, G-AFZU *Everest* and G-AFZV *Enterprise* were delivered to BOAC.

De Havilland D.H.91 Albatross Frobisher class (1938-1940)

G-AFD1	*Frobisher*	C/n 6802	C of A	17 October 1938	To BOAC.
G-AFDJ	*Falcon*	C/n 6803	C of A	1 November 1938	To BOAC.
G-AFDK	*Fortuna*	C/n 6804	C of A	6 January 1939	To BOAC.
G-AFDL	*Fingid*	C/n 6805	C of A	4 April 1939	To BOAC.
G-AFDM	*Fiona*	C/n 6806	C of A	16 June 1939	To BOAC.
G-AEVV	*Faraday*	C/n 6800		Mail carrier	To BOAC.

Saunders-Roe A.19 Cloud (1940)

G-ABHG	C/n 19/2.	C of A 31 July 1931.

For crew training January 1940. Damaged beyond repair, June 1941.

Short S.26 G class flying-boat

G-AFCI	*Golden Hind*	C/n S.871	Transferred to Air Ministry. To BOAC.
G-AFCJ	*Golden Fleece*	C/n S.872	
G-AFCK	*Golden Horn*	C/n S.873	

The G class flying-boats were built for Imperial Airways but never went into service with that airline.

eight

The Aircraft

Airco D.H.4 and D.H.4A

The D.H.4 two-seat bomber and fighter-reconnaissance biplane was one of the outstanding types produced for the 1914-1918 war. Designed by Geoffrey de Havilland at the Aircraft Manufacturing Company, the first example took its maiden flight at Hendon in August 1916.

The D.H.4 was put into production by Airco and six other United Kingdom companies which built a total of 1,449. Two examples were built in Belgium by SABCA. Five United States companies, including Boeing, built 4,587.

One problem about this large-scale production was a shortage of suitable engines and D.H.4s were powered by over twenty types of engine ranging from the 200hp RAF 3A to the 525hp Packard 2A-1500. Many of the British-built aircraft had the 325hp Rolls-Royce Eagle VII and 375hp Eagle VIII. In layout the D.H.4 was an equal-span two-bay strut and wire-braced biplane of wood and fabric construction.

In December 1918 No.1 (Communication) Squadron was formed under the command of Major Cyril Patteson and the squadron operated London (Hendon)-Paris (Buc) services for members of HM Government attending the Peace Conference. No.2 (Communication) Squadron was formed in March 1919 and, during the Conference, operated a daily courier and mail service between Kenley and BVC.

Because of the discomfort of open cockpits, Mr Bonar Law, the Prime Minister, requested that a number of Eagle VIII-powered D.H.4s be given a cabin with two facing seats so that a minister and secretary could work on the flights. Thus the D.H.4A was born. At least seven aircraft were converted for No.2 Squadron of which H5894 was lost in the English Channel.

In the D.H.4A the rear gunner's cockpit was replaced by the two-seat cabin which was covered by a hinged roof in two sections and reached via a ladder attached to the starboard side of the fuselage. Because of the weight of the extra passenger and deepened rear fuselage it was necessary to re-rig the aircraft with the wings one foot further aft and without stagger. These modifications led to the new designation D.H.4A. The conversions were made by Airco and Handley Page.

Aircraft Transport & Travel had four D.H.4As and, after one was forced down in the English Channel and another crashed, the airline replaced these with two D.H.4s. Handley Page Transport used two D.H.4As, including the first one. S. Instone & Co. had a Waring & Gillow-built D.H.4 which was converted to D.H.4A and this won the first Kings Cup race in 1922, flying from London to Glasgow and back at an average speed of 123mph. This aircraft passed to Imperial Airways but was only used as an engine test bed. SNETA in Belgium had two D.H.4As, both of which were burned in a hangar fire.

There appear to have been fifteen D.H.4As built or converted.

D.H.4.
375hp Rolls-Royce Eagle VIII

Span	42ft 4⅝in
Length	30ft 6in
Wing area	434 sq.ft
Empty weight	2,387lb
Maximum weight	3,472lb
Maximum speed	143mph
Endurance	3¾ hours

D.H.4.A
350hp Rolls-Royce Eagle VIII

Span	42ft 4⅝in
Length	30ft 6in
Wing area	434 sq.ft
Empty weight	2,600lb
Maximum weight	3,720lb
Maximum speed	121mph
Endurance	About 3 hours

Airco D.H.6

In November 1916 it was decided to increase the number of Royal Flying Corps squadrons in France from twenty-six to fifty-six. This meant that large numbers of men would have to be trained as pilots and there was a desperate need for training aircraft. To meet this need, Geoffrey de Havilland at the Aircraft Manufacturing Company designed the D.H.6 two-seat tractor biplane, which was planned for ease of manufacture, maintenance and repair. The highly cambered lower and upper wings were interchangeable and many of the aircraft's lines were straight. The prototypes had the typical de Havilland fin and rudder with their pleasing lines, but in production aircraft these surfaces had straight edges. There was a long open cockpit seating instructor and pupil.

Most D.H.6's had 90hp RAF 1a engines but 90hp Curtiss OX-5 and 80hp Renault engines were also used.

S. Instone's Waring & Gillow-built Airco D.H.4 G-EAMU at Hounslow.

F5764, the first Airco D.H.4A. This RAF Communication Squadron's aeroplane passed to Handley Page Transport as G-EAWH.

The D.H.6 had several shortcomings and a number of modifications were made including removal of 4in from the wing leading edges to reduce the camber. This ugly, but useful, aeroplane attracted numerous nicknames including the Clutching Hand, the Sky Hook, the Clockwork Mouse and the Dung Hunter. More than 2,000 D.H.6s were built by Airco and seven other British companies. One was also built in Canada.

After the war, more than fifty D.H.6s came on to the British Civil Register. Aircraft Transport & Travel had one D.H.6. It was given the temporary registration K-100 and was the first aeroplane to fly in the United Kingdom with a civil registration. It was re-registered G-EAAB and it was flown at Hendon race meetings. Some D.H.6s were also used for pleasure flights at Southport until 1933.

D.H.6
90hp RAF 1A

Span	35ft 11in
Length	27ft 3½in
Wing area	436¼ sq.ft
Empty weight	1,460lb
Maximum weight	2,027lb
Maximum speed	70mph
Endurance	2¾ hours

Airco D.H.9

In June 1917 it was decided to increase the operational strength of the Royal Flying Corps from 168 to 200 squadrons and that most of the additional strength would be bomber units. Geoffrey de Havilland modified the D.H.4 to become the D.H.9 and 700 were ordered.

It was thought that the D.H.9 would have superior performance to the D.H.4 but it proved to be inferior in most respects except range. The D.H.9 had the same wings, rear fuselage and tail unit as the D.H.4 but there were many engine problems and on the last day of the RFC's existence only thirty-three had been allotted to the RFC in France and most of the D.H.9's service was post-war. The 230hp Siddeley Puma was the most widely used engine but some had 230hp Galloway Adriatics or 260hp Fiat A.12s.

D.H.9's were built by Airco and a dozen other UK concerns and some were built in Belgium by SABCA and in Spain by Hispano-Suiza. The prototype flew in July 1917 and many D.H.4 contracts were changed to D.H.9s.

A number of D.H.9s were on the British Civil Register after the war including seventeen with Aircraft Transport & Travel, of which nine could carry a second passenger and were designated D.H.9B. Several served the de Havilland Hire Service as D.H.9 Cs with covered rear cockpits and others were operated by SNETA, Qantas, DDL-Danish Air Lines and KLM.

D.H.9.As with Liberty engines served the RAF for many years and D.H.9.Js with Armstrong Siddeley Jaguar engines remained with the de Havilland School of Flying until 1933.

An Airco D.H.6.

D.H.9.
230hp Siddeley Puma

Span	42ft 4⅝in
Length	30ft 6in
Wing area	434 sq.ft
Empty weight	2,203lb
Maximum weight	3,669lb
Maximum speed	111.5mph
Endurance	4½ hours

Airco D.H.10

The Airco D.H.10 was designed as a bomber and served the Royal Air Force under the name Amiens. It was a large wood and fabric equal-span biplane and there were several versions. The first prototype had two 230hp Siddeley Puma engines arranged as pushers between the wings and the aeroplane first flew on 4 March 1918. The second prototype, designated Amiens MkII had Rolls-Royce 360hp Eagle VIII engines installed as tractors.

The third prototype, designated Amiens MkIII, had 396hp Liberty engines and most production aircraft were powered by Liberty engines and there were a few D.H.10s with Eagle engines mounted on the lower wing.

Royal Air Force service of the D.H.10 was limited but some were based in India and Egypt.

An Airco D.H.9 of KLM. (KLM)

Two D.H.10s were used by Aircraft Transport & Travel to operate mail services between Hendon and Glasgow (Renfrew) via Newcastle in September and October 1919 because of the railway strike. These two aeroplanes were the D.H.10C prototype E5557 and G-EAJO which had been the production aeroplane E5488. This was the only known civil operation by the D.H.10 and the projected four passenger version was not built.

D.H10. MIII
Two 400hp Liberty 72

Span	65ft 6in
Length	39ft 7½in
Wing area	837½ sq.ft
Empty weight	5,585lb
Maximum weight	9,000lb
Maximum speed	129mph ★
Endurance	5¾ hours

★ Mk IIIA

Airco D.H.16

The D.H.16 was Airco's first truly civil type, although it used many components of the military D.H.9A but with enclosed cabin and widened rear fuselage. The Airco Works drawing bore the title 'D.H.16 Aerial Limousine seating pilot and four passengers' and gave the cabin dimensions as 6ft 11in in length and 3ft 3in in

Airco D.H.10 G-EAJO. (*Flight*)

width. The engine was stated to be a 322hp Rolls-Royce Eagle VII. Fuel capacity was quoted as 56-gallon main tank and 6-gallon gravity tank. Oil tank capacity was given as 6 gallons.

In layout the D.H.16 was an equal-span, two-bay, strut and wire-braced biplane with slight wing stagger. The pilot's open cockpit was between the wings immediately forward of the cabin which housed two pairs of facing seats and was enclosed by a roof hinged along its port side. Access was via a ladder attached to the starboard side of the fuselage.

The prototype first flew at Hendon in March 1919 and in the following May entered service with Aircraft Transport & Travel as K-130. It was later registered G-EACT and on 25 August 1919 operated the first scheduled cross-Channel service, from Hounslow to Paris-Le Bourget.

Nine D.H.16's were built and the last three had 450hp Napier Lion engines. One was experimentally fitted with air-brakes and flaps. On 17 May 1920, G-EALU *Arras*, flown by H. 'Jerry' Shaw inaugurated a joint Aircraft Transport & Travel/KLM service between Croydon and Amsterdam.

All but one of the D.H.16s were used by Aircraft Transport & Travel and the sixth example built went to River Plate Aviation Co. in Argentina and operated ferry services between Buenos Aires and Montevideo in Uruguay.

D.H.16.
450hp Napier Lion
Span   46ft 5⅞in
Length   31ft 9in

Wing area	489¾ sq.ft
Empty weight	3,155lb
Maximum weight	4,750lb
Maximum speed	100mph
Range	425 miles

Airco D.H.17

The Airco D.H.17 was unfortunately never built. It was an advanced design which might have been very successful if it had not been for the economic situation at that time and would almost certainly have been operated by Aircraft Transport & Travel if the airline had survived.

The D.H.17 was to have been a large twin-engine biplane which an Airco works drawing shows as having fourteen passenger seats, six each side of the main cabin with the front two facing aft plus a 3ft 6in-wide double seat in a nose cabin. There would have been full-length windows in the main cabin and a series of windows round the nose. The main and nose cabins were separated by a door and a luggage hold and there would have been a ladder leading to the open two-seat cockpit ahead of the upper wing. The fuselage would have occupied the full 10ft 9in gap between upper and lower wings. Main cabin length would have been 18ft 6in with 5ft width and 6ft 4 ½in height. The main undercarriage unit would have been semi-retractable and had large trouser-like fairings.

Planned power was two 650hp Rolls-Royce Condor water-cooled engines driving 13ft-diameter tractor airscrews. The 220-gallon fuel tank was to have been installed in the fuselage beneath the upper wing.

D.H.17
Two 650hp Rolls-Royce Condors

Span	85ft
Length	63ft 6in approx.
Wing area	1,650 sq.ft

No figures are available for projected weights and performance.

Airco D.H.18.

The prototype D.H.18 G-EARI was the last aeroplane built by the Aircraft Manufacturing Company, although constructor's numbers E.52 to E.57 were allocated to a batch of six. The five production aircraft were built by the newly founded de Havilland Aircraft Company which gave the c/ns 1-6 for the prototype and production aircraft.

The D.H.18 was an equal-span, two-bay, strut and wire-braced biplane and at the centre line the fuselage occupied the entire 6ft 6in gap between upper and lower wings. The passenger cabin had eight seats and the open cockpit was well aft of the wings. The cabin was difficult to enter, the door, on the port side, being small and of awkward shape, and the seating compounded the difficulty with two aft seats facing forward, the two forward seats facing aft and the single seats facing

Airco D.H.16 G-EACT at Hounslow. (*Flight*)

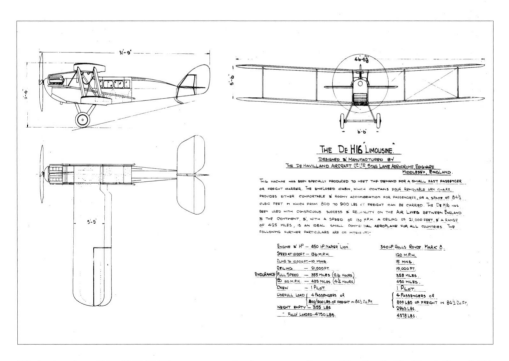

Works drawing of the D.H.16. The statement that it was manufactured by the de Havilland Aircraft Co. is wrong. It was built by Airco.

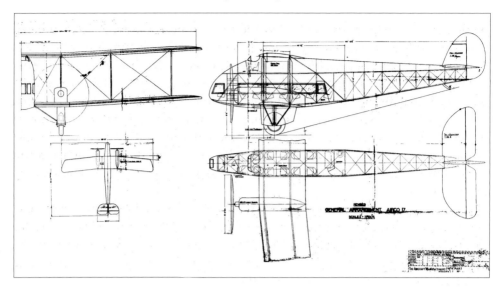

Works drawing of the projected D.H.17.

forward on the starboard side and facing aft on the port side. The structure was of wood with fabric covering and the engine was a 450hp Napier Lion.

The prototype first flew in March 1920 and entered service on the London–Paris route with Aircraft Transport & Travel in April.

The first two production aircraft, D.H.18.As with strengthened centre sections, were supplied to Instone Air Line as was the fourth aeroplane, which was built for the Air Council. The fourth aircraft passed to Daimler Airway. The last two aircraft were D.H.18Bs which had ply-covered rear fuselages and additional emergency exits. They were both used by Instone Air Line, the last being loaned to Handley Page Transport for a time in April 1922.

G-EAWW c/n 5 was finally used for ditching trials at Felixstowe in May 1924. It remained afloat for twenty-five minutes until the engine was salvaged.

D.H.18.
450hp Napier Lion

Span	51ft 2¾in
Length	39ft
Wing area	621¼sq.ft
Maximum speed	128mph
Cruising speed	100mph
Range	400 miles

Armstrong Whitworth Argosy

The Argosy was originally designed to meet a 1922 specification for a Middle East aircraft capable of flying 500 miles against a 30mph wind. Imperial Airways made an early decision to only operate multi-engine aircraft on scheduled services and finding that the Argosy would be suitable for European routes, in 1925, ordered two. The Air Ministry also ordered one. It is believed that the type's first flight was in March 1926 and Imperial Airways took delivery of the first one in July 1926.

The Argosy was a large, equal-span biplane with three 385hp Armstrong Siddeley Jaguar III air-cooled radial engines – one in the nose and two between the wings. The fuselage was of steel-tube construction and the wings were of wood, all fabric covered. There were biplane tailplanes and elevators and triple fins and rudders. The cabin was 29ft long, 4ft 6in wide and 6ft 3in high and had ten forward-facing seats on each side. There was a two-seat open cockpit high up in the nose.

The Argosy went into service on 16 July 1926 on the London-Paris route and proved to have good economics – 9*d* per ton-mile compared with 14*d* for the Handley Page W.10. From 1 May 1927, Argosies were used to operate the London-Paris *Silver Wing* lunchtime service. For this the two rear seats were removed, a buffet installed and a steward carried.

The Argosy greatly increased the airline's traffic and the airline stated that the Argosy was the first type to cover its costs, so in 1928 an order was placed for another three, later increased to four.

The second batch of Argosies, designated MKII had 410hp Jaguar IVA engines, for a while with Townend ring cowling, circular engine nacelles and servo surfaces to operate the ailerons. The original aircraft were then designated Mk.1 and

The prototype Airco D.H.18.

De Havilland D.H.18B G-EAWX of Instone Air Line.

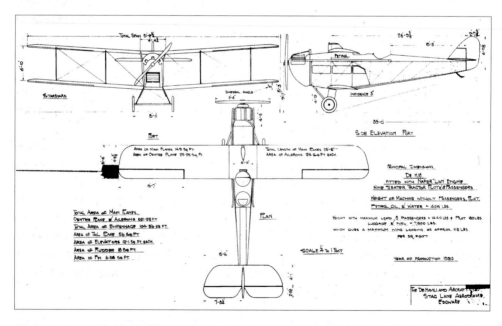

Works drawing of the de Havilland D.H.18.

were later re-engined with Jaguar VI As. Two Mk.1s were transferred to Cairo for operation on the Cairo-Khartoum section of the Africa route which was opened in March 1931. The Argosies were finally withdrawn in 1934 but several continued to be used for joy riding including one sold to United Airways for joy riding near Blackpool in 1936.

Armstrong Whitworth Argosy
Three Armstrong Siddeley Jaguars

	Mk.I	Mk.II
Span	90ft 8in	90ft 4in
Length	65ft 10in	67ft
Wing area	1,886 sq.ft	1,873 sq.ft
Empty weight		12,090lb
Loaded weight	18,000lb	19,200lb
Cruising speed	90-95mph	90-95mph
Range	330 miles	520 miles

Armstrong Whitworth A.W.XV Atalanta

The Atalanta was the first British mainline monoplane. In 1930 Imperial Airways issued a specification for an aeroplane to operate the Kisumu-Cape Town sector of the forthcoming England-South Africa service. It was stated that it should have a cruising speed of not less than 115mph, a range of 400 miles, be capable of operating from small, hot and high aerodromes, have a payload of 3,000lb and be able to maintain a height of 9,000ft with one engine shut down.

Armstrong Whitworth met this specification with an attractive high-wing cantilever monoplane of mixed construction powered by four 375hp Armstrong Siddeley Double Mongoose (later renamed Serval) air-cooled radial engines mounted on the leading edge of the wing.

There was a mail hold capable of housing a ton of mail and the passenger cabin was originally designed to have nine seats. It was furnished to make flying in the tropics as comfortable as possible and the walls were painted yellow in the belief that this would keep flies off. The first example flew on 6 June 1932 and was followed by another seven, two of which were allocated to Indian Trans-Continental Airways. For a short time from September 1932 the type operated European services after which they worked between Kisumu and Cape Town in Africa and eastwards from Karachi, finally as far as Singapore. The five surviving aircraft passed to BOAC in 1940.

Armstrong Whitworth A.W.XV Atalanta
Four 375hp Armstrong Siddeley Servals

Span	90ft
Length	71ft 6in
Wing area	1,285 sq.ft

An Imperial Airways Armstrong Whitworth Argosy in original blue and silver livery.

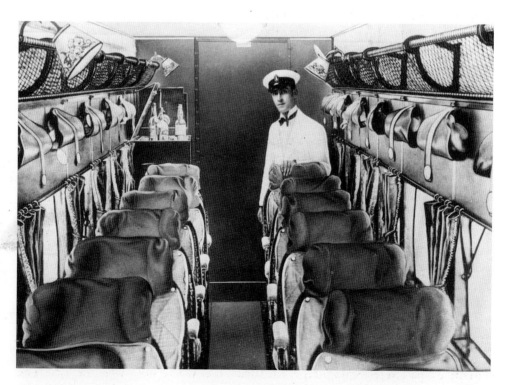

The cabin of an Argosy.

Imperial Airways Armstrong Whitworth Argosy Mk.II *City of Edinburgh* in front of the then new Croydon Airport Terminal. (*The Aeroplane*)

Empty weight	14,832lb
Maximum weight	21,000lb
Maximum speed	156mph
Cruising speed	118mph
Range	640 miles

Armstrong Whitworth A.W.27 Ensign

In December 1934, HM Government announced the Empire Air Mail Programme stating that 'beginning in 1937 all letters despatched from the United Kingdom for delivery along the Empire routes would, so far as was practicable, be carried by air without surcharge'. To meet the anticipated loads Imperial Airways ordered a large fleet of Short Empire flying-boats but also saw the need for a European and Empire landplane.

To satisfy the requirement for the landplane Armstrong Whitworth produced plans for high and low-wing monoplanes with three and four engines. The four-engined high-wing A.W.27 was chosen and orders for twelve were placed and the class name Ensign was given to it. There were numerous delays in its production mostly caused by the re-armament programme and the first A.W.27 did not fly until 24 January 1938.

The Ensign was produced in two versions, the 40-passenger European model and the 27-passenger Empire type. Externally the two versions were identical. The engines were 800hp Armstrong Siddeley Tiger IXs and with these engines the Ensign was underpowered. This type also suffered from undercarriage problems.

Armstrong Whitworth A.W.XV *Athena* at Karachi.

Limited operations began on the London–Paris route at the end of 1938 by which time a further two aeroplanes had been ordered. Four of the Ensigns were allotted to Indian Trans-Continental Airways but never delivered. The type was used to carry the heavy Christmas mail on the Australia route but none got further than India.

The more powerful 850hp Tiger IXC began to be installed in 1939 and, after the aircraft passed to BOAC, 950hp Wright Cyclones were fitted. Some aircraft were lost early in the war and one captured by the Germans was fitted with Daimler-Benz liquid-cooled engines.

The surviving aircraft were all broken up in 1947.

Armstrong Whitworth A.W.27
Four 850hp Armstrong Siddeley Tiger 1XC

Span	123 ft
Length	114 ft
Wing area	2,450 sq.ft
Empty weight	32,920lb
Maximum weight	48,500lb
Maximum speed	200mph
Cruising speed	170mph
Range	860 miles

With Cyclone engines the maximum weight was 55,500 lbs.

The cabin of an Armstrong Whitworth A.W.XV *Atalanta*. (Armstrong Whitworth)

Armstrong Whitworth A.W.27 *Ensign*. (*Flight*)

Left: An Avro 504K. (R.A. Cole)

Below: Avro 563 Andover. (Avro)

Avro 504K

The first Avro 504 flew as early as 1913; there were numerous versions and in February 1918 it was decided to make the Avro 504K the sole military trainer. All versions of this wood and fabric biplane up to the 504K had rotary engines but the 504N, which became the standard RAF trainer had stationary air-cooled radials and a new undercarriage dispensing with most of the earlier versions front skid.

Avro 504Ks were built in large numbers in the United Kingdom, Belgium, Canada, Denmark and Thailand. Large numbers were on the UK civil register and they operated pleasure flights well into the 1930s.

For some reason Aircraft Transport & Travel had four Avro 504Ks but it is not known what use was made of them.

Avro 504K.
130hp Clerget

Span	36ft
Length	29ft 5ins
Wing area	330 sq.ft
Empty weight	1,231lb
Maximum weight	1,829lb
Maximum speed	95mph
Cruising speed	75 mph
Range	225 miles

Avro 563 Andover

The Andover was a large single-engine biplane of mixed construction. It was intended as the Type 561, to operate the Cairo-Baghdad desert air mail route but because Imperial Airways was to take over the route only three military Andovers were built.

The Andover had two-bay folding wings, the oval-section cabin was a wooden monocoque structure and the rear fuselage was of tubular-steel with fabric covering. The passenger cabin was 22ft long, 4ft 9in wide and 6ft high. It could accommodate twelve passengers or six stretchers. There was an open cockpit for two beneath the leading edge of the centre section. The engine was a 650hp Rolls-Royce Condor III. In 1925, the Air Ministry ordered the purely civilian type 563 Andover and, after its tests in March 1925, it was lent to Imperial Airways for cross-Channel proving flights. Its certificate of airworthiness was issued on 21 April 1925 and the aeroplane went to the Royal Air Force in January 1927 as J7264.

Avro 563 Andover
650 hp Rolls-Royce Condor III

Span	68ft (folded 27ft 6in)
Length	51ft 7in
Wing area	1,064 sq.ft

Empty weight	6,800lb
Maximum weight	10,685lb
Maximum speed	110mph
Cruising speed	90mph
Range	460 miles approx

Avro Ten (Type 618)

In 1929 Avro began production of fourteen Avro Tens which were licence-produced Fokker F.VIIb/3ms. The Ten in the designation representing the eight passengers and two crew. The Avro Ten, like the Fokker, was a high-wing, cantilever monoplane with three engines. The fuselage was a fabric-covered, welded steel tube structure and the thick-section, one-piece wing was a ply-covered wooden structure. The engines chosen for the British aircraft were 240hp Armstrong Siddeley Lynx IVB and IVC air-cooled radials.

Fourteen Avro Tens were built, with five for Australian National Airways. One went to Indian National Airways, while Midlands & Scottish Air Ferries had one, and two went to Imperial Airways. The last one built was delivered to the Wireless & Equipment Flight at the Royal Aircraft Establishment at Farnborough in July 1936.

Imperial Airways took delivery of G-AASP *Achilles* in April 1931 and G-ABLU *Apollo* that June. They went on short-term charter to Iraq Petroleum Transport for desert pipeline patrol and returned to the United Kingdom in 1933 for charter use. *Apollo* struck a radio mast in Belgium while working a Brussels-London service in December 1933 and was destroyed and *Achilles* passed to BOAC.

Avro Ten
Three 240hp Armstrong Siddeley Lynx

Span	71ft 3in
Length	47ft 6in
Wing area	722 sq.ft
Empty weight	6,020lb
Maximum weight	10,600lb
Maximum speed	115mph
Cruising speed	100mph
Range	400 miles

Avro 652

In May 1933 Imperial Airways submitted a specification to Avro for a small, fast, long-range charter aircraft and in answer Avro produced the Type 652. The Avro 652 continued the Fokker tradition with fabric-covered, steel-tube fuselage and one-piece, all-wood wing but the wing was changed from high position to low. The aircraft was powered by two Armstrong Siddeley Cheetah radial engines and had a retractable undercarriage, the first on an Imperial Airways aeroplane. There was accommodation for four passengers and two crew.

Avro Ten (Type 618) *Achilles.* (Avro)

The cabin of an Avro Ten.

Avro 652 *Avalon*.

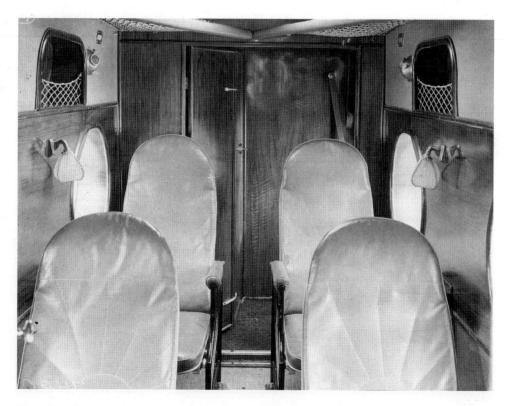

The cabin of an Avro 652. (*The Aeroplane*)

The first Avro 652 flew on 7 January 1935 and the only two aircraft of this type were delivered to Imperial Airways on 11 March 1935 as *Avalon* and *Avatar*, the latter soon being changed to *Ava*. Both passed to Air Service Training in July 1938.

While the Avro 652 was in the design stage, the Air Ministry asked Avro to tender for a coastal patrol aircraft. The design closely resembled the 652 and was put into production as the Avro 652A Anson Mk1 and several thousand were built of the numerous versions. Many were built in Canada.

Avro 652
Two 270hp Armstrong Siddeley Cheetah V

Span	56ft 6in
Length	42ft 3in
Wing area	463 sq.ft
Empty weight	5,100lb
Maximum weight	7,400lb
Maximum speed	195mph
Cruising speed	165mph
Range	790 miles

B.A.T. F.K.26

The first truly civil aeroplane built in Britain after the First World War was the British Air Transport Company's F.K.26 single-engined four passenger biplane designed by Frederick Koolhoven and built of wood. The F.K.26 first flew in April 1919 and was for a time used on the London-Paris route. On 30 September 1919 it was supposed to have started operating a twice-daily London (Hendon)-Birmingham service but only that day's flight is known. From 7 October that year it was used on a weekly Hendon-Amsterdam service but this operation ended in 1920.

In layout the F.K.26 was an equal-span two-bay strut and wire-braced biplane with a deep fuselage, the 8ft-long four-seat cabin between the wings and the pilot's open cockpit well aft towards the tail. The engine was a 350hp water-cooled Rolls-Royce Eagle VIII. Only four F.K.26s were built and the fourth aeroplane went to S. Instone & Co in August 1920. It was named *City of Newcastle* and operated between London and Paris and was used for charters. It crashed at Croydon on 31 July 1922.

The first three aircraft were stored for many years and in 1937 Koolhoven purchased the prototype and had it taken to the Netherlands.

B.A.T. FK.26
350hp Rolls-Royce Eagle VIII

Span	46ft
Length	34ft 8in
Maximum weight	4,500lb

Boulton Paul P.71A *Britomart* at Croydon.

The cabin of a Boulton Paul P.71A. (*The Aeroplane*)

Maximum speed	122mph
Cruising speed	100mph
Range	600 miles

Boulton Paul P.71A

In 1928, the Air Ministry issued a specification for a high-speed mail aircraft for use by Imperial Airways and Boulton & Paul (soon to be Boulton Paul) built the P.64 to meet this specification. It had a top speed of 185mph but crashed while on test.

In May 1933, Imperial Airways stated its requirement for a six/seven-seat aircraft for charter work and use on low-traffic feeder routes. Boulton Paul developed its ill-fated P.64 mail carrier into the P.71A and Imperial Airways bought two – *Boadicea* and *Britomart*.

These were twin-engine biplanes of mixed construction with two 490hp Armstrong Siddeley Jaguar VIA radial engines carried by the upper wing and closely cowled. The wide-track main undercarriage units were carried by the lower wing and the wheels were endorsed in large fairings. There was a central tail fin and two balanced rudders. The cabin was luxuriously fitted out and contained six fixed seats and a seventh seat, which folded against the rear bulkhead.

The two aircraft were delivered in January and February 1935 but were short-lived. *Britomart* was written off in a landing accident at Brussels on 25 October 1935 and *Boadicea* was lost in the English Channel on 25 September 1936 while engaged on a cargo flight.

Boulton Paul P.71A
Two 490 hp Armstrong Siddeley Jaguar VIA

Span	54ft 1½in
Length	44ft 2in
Wing area	718 sq.ft
Empty weight	6,700lb
Loaded weight	9,500lb
Maximum speed	195mph
Cruising speed	145-150mph
Range	600 miles

Bristol 47 Tourer

In January 1919 the Controller of Civil Aviation requested that three Bristol F.2B Fighters be delivered as two-seat communications aeroplanes. This led to production of several types under the designation Tourer. These were two- and three-seat open and coupé types and the three seaters had widened rear fuselages to seat two passengers side-by-side. There was also a twin-float seaplane version.

Only one Tourer was operated by a British airline, that was the Type 47 G-EART open cockpit three-seater that was supplied to S. Instone & Co., it was used for charter work. Another four were delivered to the USA and three went to Spain.

S. Instone & Co.'s Bristol 47 Tourer. (Bristol Aeroplane Co.)

In Australia, Western Australia Airways had six Bristol Tourers and used them on the county's first subsidised air service – from Geraldton to Derby, but the Tourer operating the service on 5 December 1921 crashed.

An unusual feature of the Tourer and the Fighter before it was the gap between the bottom of the fuselage and the lower wing.

Bristol 47 Tourer
230hp Siddeley Puma

Span	39ft 5in
Length	26ft 1in
Wing area	407 sq.ft
Empty weight	1,900lb
Loaded weight	3,000lb
Maximum speed	117mph
Range	400 miles

Bristol Ten-seater

The title Ten-seater was derived from pilot and nine passengers, which the type could carry. The Ten-seater was a large single-engine, two-bay biplane with the fuselage occupying the complete gap between the wings. The first example, the Type 62, flew in June 1921 and was lent to Handley Page Transport for use on a London–Cologne cargo service. This version had a 450hp Napier Lion engine with the fuel tanks beneath the lower wing. It had a well-appointed cabin with large windows and the pilot's open cockpit was ahead of the upper wing.

The Type 62 was followed by the Type 75 425 hp Bristol Jupiter IV air-cooled radial engine and seats for eight passengers and two crew. It was first flown in July 1922 and under the name Bristol Pullman it was bought by Instone Airline. As its C of A was not awarded until July 1924, Instone had by then been absorbed by Imperial Airways. The new airline set a policy of only using multi-engine aircraft for passenger carriage on scheduled services and so the Ten-seater was converted to Type 75A Express Freight Carrier and put into service on the London-Cologne route on 22 July 1924. The Types 62 and 75 were very similar but the latter had its fuel tanks transferred to the upper wing.

Bristol Ten-Seater Types 62 and 75

450hp Napier Lion		425hp Bristol Jupiter IV	
Span	54ft 3in	Span	56ft
Length	42ft	Length	40ft 6in
Wing area	685 sq.ft	Wing area	700 sq.ft
Empty weight	3,900lb	Empty weight	4,000lb
Loaded weight	6,800lb	Loaded weight	6,755lb
Maximum speed	122mph	Maximum speed	110mph
Endurance	5½hr	Endurance	5½hr

Bristol Type 62 ten-seater. (Bristol Aeroplane Co.)

The Bristol Type 75 after conversion to Type 75A Express Freighter. (Bristol Aeroplane Co.)

De Havilland D.H.34

The Aircraft Manufacturing Co. was sold to the Birmingham Small Arms Co. (BSA) and soon afterwards BSA closed Airco. So Geoffrey de Havilland founded the de Havilland Aircraft Co. on 25 September 1920 with some financial help from George Holt Thomas. The new company completed five D.H.18s (see Airco D.H.18) and then embarked on an improved type. This first attempt was the D.H.32 with many of the D.H.18's successful features but with the cockpit moved from the cabin to just forward of the upper wing and all eight passenger seats facing forward. The proposed engine was a special commercial version of the 360hp Rolls Royce Eagle.

It was announced in September 1921 that construction of the D.H.32 was about to begin but potential customers wanted an aeroplane with the 450hp Napier Lion and the D.H.32 was further refined as the Lion-powered D.H.34 for nine passengers and two crew.

The D.H.34 was a wood and fabric, two-bay biplane and both Instone Air Line and Daimler Airway placed orders for a total of ten. The first flight took place on 26 March 1922 with A.J. (later Sir Alan) Cobham as pilot and almost unbelievably the type entered service with Daimler on the London-Paris route on 2 April although its Certificate of Airworthiness and those of the next four were not issued until 6 May.

The passenger cabin was 15ft 5in long and 4ft wide and it had four forward-facing seats each side and a ninth seat right aft on the port side beside the lavatory. Aft of the bulkhead was a baggage compartment. A communicating door in the ront bulkhead led to the cockpit which was reached from the outside by a ladder attached to the port side. There were fresh-air controls above the full-length windows. The passengers' entrance was on the starboard side.

The span on a November 1921 works drawing is given as 50ft 6in and chord 5ft 9in but the span is believed to have been increased to 51ft 4in. Undercarriage track was 7ft 9in. There was a 40-gallon. fuel tank on each side below the upper wing. The D.H.34 had a fairly high stalling speed and several were given 3ft increase in span and 6in in chord. These were redesignated D.H.34B.

Daimler Airway had six D.H.34s and Instone Air Line four and one was sold to the Soviet airline Dobrojet.

The D.H.34 soon earned an outstanding reputation for reliability and Daimler's G-EBBS was the first aeroplane to make two London-Paris-London flights in one day and this achievement was repeated more than forty times. G-EBBS was finally written off when, on 14 September 1923, it crashed at Ivinghoe Beacon, Bucks, while operating a Manchester-London flight. Daimler's G-EBBU had another aircraft land on top of it at Croydon but was rebuilt. Four Instone and three Daimler D.H.34s were taken over by Imperial Airways in 1924 but all survivors were scrapped by 1926 with some of their engines being used to power the new Handley Page W.10s.

De Havilland D.H.34
450hp Napier Lion

Span	51ft 4in (54ft 4in D.H.34B)
Length	39ft
Wing area	590 sq.ft (637sq.ft D.H.34B)
Empty weight	4,574lb (4,674lb D.H.34B)
Loaded weight	7,200lb
Maximum speed	128mph
Cruising speed	105mph (100mph D.H.34B)
Range	365 miles

De Havilland D.H.50

The D.H.50 was a four-passenger, two-bay biplane designed to replace the de Havilland Hire Services D.H.9Cs. The cabin with folding roof was between the wings with the pilot's open cockpit further aft.

The prototype first flew on 30 July 1923 and four days later Alan Cobham flew it to Gothenburg for the International Aeronautical Exhibition where it won first prize in the reliability trial which involved flying between Gothenburg and Copenhagen every day from 7 to 12 August. The prototype and several others had the 230hp Siddeley Puma engine.

The second and third aircraft were delivered to Imperial Airways for charter work. The second, G-EBFO, at one time with full-span flaps on both wings, was used to make several route surveys. Between 10 November 1924 and 17 March 1925, Alan Cobham flew Sir Sefton Brancker on a survey flight to India and

An Imperial Airways de Havilland D.H.34.

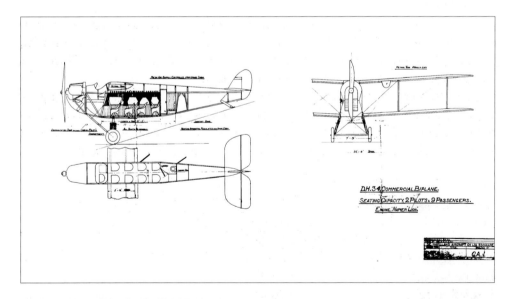

Works drawing of the de Havilland D.H.34.

An Imperial Airways de Havilland D.H.50.

Burma – 18,000 miles in 210 hours – with an Armstrong Siddeley Jaguar radial engine. G-EBFO was also flown by Cobham to Cape Town, leaving Stag Lane on 16 November 1925.

The D.H.50 was then fitted with twin floats by Short Bros and, again with Cobham as pilot, it left Rochester on 30 June 1926 on a survey flight to Australia, reaching Melbourne on 15 August. On its return it alighted on the Thames at Westminster, completing 28,000 miles in 78 days.

D.H.50s were widely used in Australia, mostly D.H.50Js with Bristol Jupiter engines, and the type was built by Qantas, West Australian Airways and the Larkin Supply Company. D.H.50s were also built by SABCA in Belgium and by Aero in Czechoslovakia. The total number is believed to have been thirty-eight.

De Havilland D.H.50
230hp Siddeley Puma

Span	42ft 9in
Length	29ft 9in
Wing area	434 sq.ft
Empty weight	2,253lb
Loaded weight	3,900lb
Maximum speed	112mph
Cruising speed	95mph
Range	380 miles

D.H.50 G-EBFO, with Jaguar engine and twin floats. Alighting at Westminster on 1 October 1926 on its return flight from Australia.

De Havilland D.H.54 Highclere

Because of the success of the D.H.34s the Air Ministry issued specification 40/22 for a similar but larger successor with certain refinements, some of which were to meet lessons learned from the ditching trials with the D.H.18 (see Airco D.H.18).

To meet the specification de Havilland designed and built the D.H.54 Highclere. It was a large single-engine biplane with accommodation for twelve passengers and two crew. There were four single seats on the starboard side which contained the door and four double seats on the port side. The open cockpit was under the leading edge of the upper wing. Structure was similar to that of the D.H.34.

The engine was a 650hp Rolls Royce Condor IIIA. It drove a four-blade airscrew and had a Bristol gas starter because the airscrew was too high for hand swinging. Cabin heating was drawn from a muff round the exhaust pipe. Sliding windows could be opened. To meet the possibility of a forced landing on water the undercarriage could be jettisoned and the bottom of the fuselage and the cabin door were watertight. Full-span automatic camber-changing flaps reduced the landing speed to 52mph.

The Highclere first flew on 28 May 1925 and the Certificate of Airworthiness was awarded on 23 April 1926, by which time Imperial Airways had decided only to use multi-engine aircraft on passenger services. The Highclere, however, was delivered to Imperial Airways for use on freight services and the aeroplane was damaged beyond repair at Croydon in February 1927 when its hangar collapsed under the weight of snow.

The de Havilland D.H.54 *Highclere*.

De Havilland D.H.54 Highclere
650hp Rolls-Royce Condor IIIA

Span	68ft 2in
Length	51ft
Wing area	1,004 sq.ft
Empty weight	6,768lb
Loaded weight	11,250lb
Maximum speed	110mph
Cruising speed	100mph
Range	400 miles

De Havilland D.H.61 Giant Moth

The D.H.61 Giant Moth, for a time called *Canberra* was built in 1927 to meet an Australian requirement for a D.H.50J replacement. It was a fairly large, single-engine biplane normally powered by a Bristol Jupiter air-cooled radial engine and accommodating six-to-eight passengers.

The type first flew in December 1927 and ten were built, of which five were employed in Australia and four in Canada, of which two were twin-float seaplanes.

One Giant Moth, G-AAEV *Youth of Britain*, went to Alan Cobham Aviation and in 1929 Sir Alan Cobham took it on a tour of the United Kingdom in an attempt to get municipalities to build aerodromes. During the tour, Cobham

De Havilland D.H.61 Giant Moth *Youth of Britain*.

flew about 3,500 mayors and members of corporations and some 10,000 school children.

The *Youth of Britain* was then flown to Salisbury, Southern Rhodesia (now Harare in Zimbabwe), where Cobham delivered it to Imperial Airways on 7 January 1930. On 19 January, it was wrecked in a crash landing at Broken Hill.

De Havilland D.H.61 Giant Moth
450 hp Bristol Jupiter VI ★

Span	52ft
Length	38ft 9in
Wing area	613 sq.ft
Empty weight	3,465lb
Loaded weight	6,200lb
Maximum speed	126mph
Cruising speed	105mph
Range	475 miles

★550hp Bristol Jupiter XIF, 500hp Armstrong Siddeley Jaguar VIC and 525hp Pratt & Whitney Hornet engines were also used.

De Havilland D.H.66 Hercules

The D.H.66 Hercules was a large three-engine two-bay biplane designed for operation on Imperial Airways route to India. Five aircraft were originally ordered and the first flew on 30 September 1926.

The wings were of wood but, unlike previous de Havilland types, the Hercules had a fuselage of tubular steel construction. The cabin, originally for eight passengers, was a wooden box with full-length windows. The open cockpit was at a higher level just forward of the cabin. The engines were three 420hp Bristol Jupiter VI air-cooled radials and the wide-track undercarriage consisted of single wheels and there was a tailskid. The tail unit was unusual with a second tailplane mounted above the triple fins. There were three rudders.

The first Hercules left for Cairo on 20 December 1926 and the second aircraft made a flight to India. The first section of Imperial Airways Empire routes was opened on 7 January 1927 when the first Hercules left Basra for Baghdad and Cairo. The entire route did not open until 1929, mainly due to political difficulties.

In Australia, West Australian Airways received a subsidy for a Perth-Adelaide service and selected the Hercules to operate it. Four aircraft were purchased and these had enclosed cockpits and tailwheels which were soon replaced by skids. The total number of Hercules was eleven.

Imperial Airways *City of Teheran* crashed at Gaza in February 1930 and one of the Australian aircraft was acquired to replace it. Eventually Imperial Airways obtained two more of the Australian Hercules to replace losses. In January 1932, Imperial Airways extended its England-Central Africa route to Cape Town and Hercules were used on the new sector until replaced by the Atalanta monoplanes. The surviving Imperial Airways Hercules mostly went to the South African Air Force, two remaining in service until 1943.

De Havilland D.H.66 Hercules
Three 420hp Bristol Jupiter VI

Span	79ft 6in
Length	55ft 6in
Wing area	1,547 sq.ft
Empty weight	9,060lb
Loaded weight	15,660lb
Maximum speed	128mph
Cruising speed	110mph
Range	400 miles approx.

De Havilland D.H.86

The D.H.86 was designed in 1933 to meet an Australian Government specification for a ten-passenger aeroplane capable of safely operating the Brisbane-Singapore section of the soon to come England-Australia air route.

The aircraft, which first flew on 14 January 1934, was a wood and fabric biplane with finely tapered wings and four 200hp de Havilland Gipsy Six engines. The main undercarriage units were in fairings beneath the inboard engines. The first four aircraft had short noses with only the pilot's seat in the cockpit but subsequent aeroplanes had lengthened noses and two-seat cockpits. Qantas Empire Airways had six D.H.86s and Holyman's Airways used the type on Melbourne-Hobart services.

De Havilland D.H.66 Hercules *City of Teheran*.

Imperial Airways operated twelve as the Diana class. They served European routes and also the feeder services from Khartoum to West Africa and from Penang and Bangkok to Hong Kong. Railway Air Services used D.H.86s to open the London–Glasgow Royal Mail route, Hillman's Airways and British Airways Ltd used the type as did Blackpool & West Coast Air Services, Jersey Airways, Allied Airways and Union Airways in New Zealand. Mist Airwork in Egypt, THY in Turkey and PLUNA in Uruguay were all users of the D.H.86.

With a change in cockpit window angle the type became the D.H.86A. The final production aircraft had end-plate fins on the tailplanes and were designated D.H.86B. Most D.H.86As were converted to D.H.86B standard. Sixty-two D.H.86s were built and several survived to operate services after the Second World War, including Railway Air Services' short-nose *Mercury*.

De Havilland D.H.86
Four 200 or 205hp de Havilland Gipsy Six

	D.H.86 (2 pilots)	D.H.86B
Span	64ft 6in	64ft 6in
Length	46ft 1in	46ft 1in
Wing area	641 sq.ft	641 sq.ft
Empty weight	6,303lb	6,489lb
Loaded weight	10,000lb	10,250lb
Maximum speed	170mph	166mph
Cruising speed	145mph	142mph
Range	760 miles	800 miles

★ The short-nose aeroplanes had a length of 43ft 11in.

1 de Havilland D.H. 34 of Daimler Airway.

2 Handley Page W.8 Type.

3 de Havilland D.H. 66 Hercules *City of Delhi*.

4 An Armstrong Whitworth Argosy and a Fokker F.VII.

5 The Instone Air Line Vickers Vimy
Commercial *City of London*.

6 The Short Calcutta *City of Alexandria*.

7 Short L.17 Seylla.

8 A page of an Imperial Airways Combined Machines folder.

9 Another page from a Combined Machines folder.

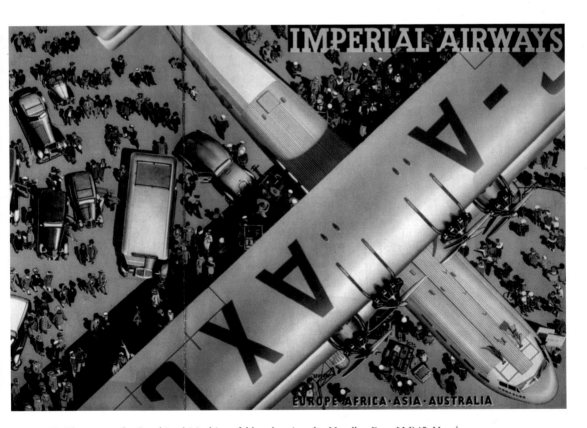

10 The cover of a Combined Machines folder, showing the Handley Page H.P.45 *Heracles*.

11 Imperial Airways publication showing *Canopus* on the cover.

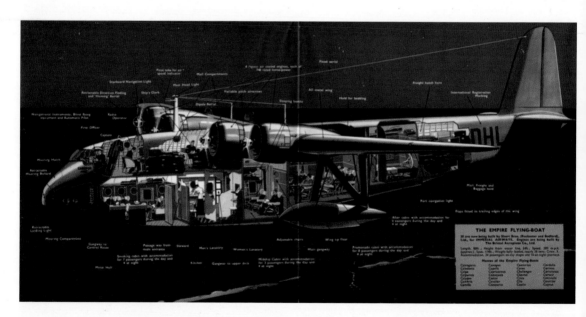

12 Section drawing of *Canopus*.

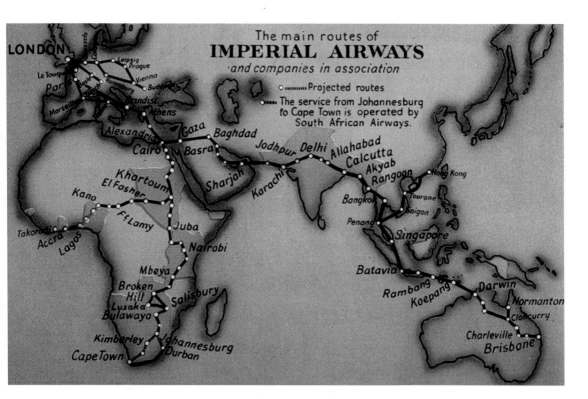

13 Imperial Airways route map.

14 Painting of *Canopus*, by Norman Wilkinson.

15 Armstrong Whitworth Atlanta.

atalanta

16 Short C class flying-boat *Cambria*.

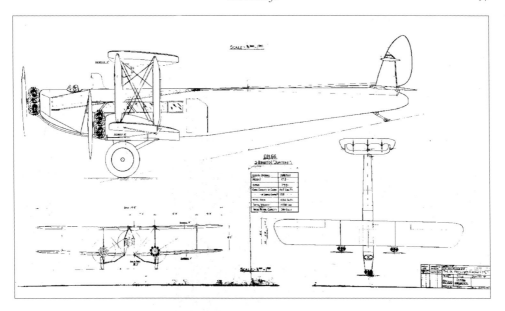

Works drawing of the de Havilland D.H.66 Hercules.

De Havilland D.H.91 Albatross Frobisher Class

The D.H.91 Albatross was a truly beautiful aeroplane with finely tapered wing and circular-section streamlined fuselage. It was the first British airliner capable of cruising at more than 200mph but unfortunately only seven were built, the Second World War prevented the type achieving its full potential. The Albatross was an all-wood aeroplane with low wing, retractable undercarriage, twin fins and rudders and four specially designed 525hp de Havilland Gipsy Twelve engines. The fuselage was of stressed-skin construction with inner and outer layers of cedar ply and between them a core of balsa. The one-piece wing, with marked dihedral, was of wood with spruce plank covering.

There was accommodation for twenty-two passengers in three cabins with floor widths ranging from 7ft to 8ft 4in and headroom from 6ft 3in to 6ft 6in. There were two lavatories aft and mail, freight and baggage holds fore and aft. Five of the D.H.91s were built as passenger aircraft for Imperial Airways and two were built to Air Ministry Specification 36/35 as experimental transatlantic mail carriers capable of carrying a 1,000lb payload for 2,500 miles at 210mph against a 40mph headwind.

The first flight was made on 20 May 1937 by the first of the two long-range aeroplanes. The first Imperial Airways' aircraft, *Frobisher*, was delivered in October 1938 and, on 23 November, it flew from Croydon to Le Bourget in fifty-three minutes. Ad hoc services were operated from the end of 1938. In December *Frobisher* and *Falcon* carried Christmas mail as far as Alexandria and in January 1939 *Falcon* flew to Marseilles in three hours and to Brussels in forty-eight minutes.

Imperial Airways made some experimental flights with the first long-range aeroplane which was given the name *Faraday*. The second long-range aeroplane was named *Franklin* but it did not get its C of A until July 1940.

De Havilland D.H.86 *Delphinus* with original single-seat nose.

De Havilland D.H.86 *Draco* with lengthened two-seat nose.

The Imperial Airways aircraft all passed to BOAC.

De Havilland D.H.91 Albatross
Four 525hp de Havilland Gipsy Twelve

Span	104ft 8in
Length	70ft
Wing area	1,078 sq.ft
Empty weight	20,298lb
Loaded weight	29,500lb
Maximum speed	225mph
Cruising speed	210mph
Range	1,040 miles

Desoutter I

The Desoutter was a licence-built Koolhoven F.K.41 three-seat high-wing monoplane of wooden construction with fabric-covered wing. The second example had modified engine cowling and lowered tailplane and was exhibited at the 1929 Olympic Aero Show as the Desoutter Dolphin. Twenty-eight Desoutters were built, of which three were exported.

The first Desoutters were followed in 1930 by the improved Desoutter II and the earlier aircraft were then designated Desoutter I. National Flying Services had nineteen orange and black, Hermes-engined Desoutters and the first Desoutter II with a de Havilland Gipsy III engine did joyriding at Croydon for Rollason Aircraft Services. There were thirteen Desoutter IIs of which seven were exported. The British Red Cross Society had two Desoutter Is but when the society closed its Aviation Department one went to Imperial Airways as Air Taxi No.6

Desoutter I
One 105 or 115hp Cirrus Hermes

Span	36ft
Length	27ft
Wing area	190 sq.ft
Empty weight	1,100lb
Loaded weight	1,900lb
Maximum speed	115mph
Cruising speed	97mph
Range	400 miles

Handley Page O/400 Series

The O/400 was a large twin-engine bomber developed from the O/100 supplied to the Royal Naval Air Service in 1915-1917, the O/100 making its first flight on 17 December 1915. The O/400 was intended for the Royal Flying Corps but seems to have been too late for that service and was delivered to the Royal Air Force.

De Havilland D.H.91 Albatross *Frobisher* over Croydon Airport.

The very clean lines of the De Havilland D.H.91 Albatross. (*Flight*)

One of the two long-range de Havilland D.H.91s. (*Flight*)

View from the front cabin of a de Havilland D.H.91 Frobisher class *Albatross*.

Desoutter I G–ABMW at Croydon.

No.1 (Communication) Squadron had eight O/400s and used them from January 1919 on Hendon-Buc flights in connection with the Peace Conference. Two or three were equipped as VIP aircraft, one with six seats and large windows and one with eight seats and four small windows.

Handley Page was awarded a military contract to build 324 O/400s of which 211 were delivered and 113 cancelled. Production by other companies brought the total to more than 500. When civil flying was allowed in the United Kingdom from May 1919 Handley Page made a series of flights with O/400s dropping newspapers by parachute to as far north as Aberdeen.

On 14 June 1919 Handley Page Transport was incorporated as a subsidiary of the manufacturer, Handley Page acquired sixteen O/400s, four of which had been completed and twelve uncompleted. Four of these were awarded the first Certificates of Airworthiness. The fuel tanks were in the fuselage and seven seats were installed fore and aft of the tanks. Two more passengers could be carried in the former nose gunner's open cockpit. The interiors were also obstructed by cross-bracing tie-rods. Handley Page then built eleven O/7s which had many improvements. The fuel tanks were positioned at the rear of the engine nacelles and the tie-rods replaced with diagonal tubular struts which were less of an obstruction. There were eight windows in each side of the cabin which was 15ft 6in long, 6ft 2in high and had a maximum width of 4ft 8in. A works drawing shows three seats on the port side and four on the starboard. In front of this cabin was a baggage hold and forward of this a 7ft 3in-long four-seat cabin. Handley Page exported six O/7s to China and four to H.P. Indo-Burmese Transport in India and converted one of Handley Page Transport's O/400s to this standard. For a short time the O/7 was known as the O.700. Handley Page Transport also had three O/11 freighters and ten O/10s which were O/11s converted to O/7 standard.

Regular services were begun between Cricklewood and Paris via Hounslow on 2 September 1919. The standard engine was the 360hp Rolls-Royce VIII, although one example had 450hp Napier Lion IIs and one O/10 was tested with 436hp Bristol Jupiter IV air-cooled radials.

The O/10 G-EATH inaugurated a thrice-weekly London-Paris-Basle-Zürich service as late as 16 August 1923 and this aeroplane passed to Imperial Airways in 1924 but was never used.

Handley Page O/400
Two 360hp Rolls-Royce Eagle VIII

Span	100ft
Length	62ft 10¼in
Wing area	1,648 sq.ft
Empty weight	8.326lb
Loaded weight	12,050lb
Maximum speed	97.5mph
Cruising speed	70mph approx.
Range	About 500 miles

Handley Page W.8

The W.8 was built in 1919 and first flew on 2 December. It was an equal-span biplane with folding wings and, unlike previous Handley Page types, had a completely unobstructed interior. The cabin was well-appointed with wall-to-wall carpet and there were sixteen forward-facing seats each with its own circular window. Port-holes in the floor for downward view were soon deleted. The engines in nacelles between the wings were two 450hp Napier Lions. Small gravity fuel tanks were beneath the upper wing.

On 4 December 1919, the W.8 was flown to Paris for the VIe Exposition Internationale de Locomotion Aérenne, by which time the rudder height had been reduced. On 4 May 1920, the W.8 was flown for one hour twenty minutes to a height of nearly 14,000ft with a load of water ballast equal to twenty-six passengers and, on 21 October 1920, named *Newcastle*, it entered service with Handley Page Transport on the London-Paris route but its seating was reduced to twelve. The W.8 was used for trials to provide performance data for the projected W.8bs. The projected W.8a with Cosmos Jupiter radial engines was never built

The W.8,. by then renamed *Duchess of York*, was written off after a crash landing at Poix in northern France on 10 July 1923.

Handley Page W.8
Two 450hp Napier Lion IB

Span	75ft
Length	60ft 3in
Wing area	1,450 sq.ft
Empty weight	8,000lb
Loaded weight	12,250lb
Maximum speed	115mph
Cruising speed	90mph
Range	500 miles

Handley Page W.8b

The W.8b may well be considered to be the production version of the W.8 with two Rolls-Royce Eagle VIII engines, full-length cabin windows and accommodation for twelve passengers (later increased to fourteen). The wings did not fold and the fuel tanks were mounted on the upper wing.

Handley Page Transport had three W.8bs, while one was built by Handley Page for Sabena and a further three for Sabena were built in Belgium by SABCA.

W.8bs began operation of the London-Paris services on 4 May 1922. Originally named *Bombay* and *Melbourne*, the first two were renamed *Princess Mary* and *Prince George* and the third example was *Prince Henry*. All three were taken over by Imperial Airways. The first aircraft crashed at Abbeville in February 1928, *Prince George* was withdrawn from use in April 1929 and *Prince Henry* in March 1932. The last was thereafter used for joy riding.

Handley Page Transport' O/400 D.8350 became G-EAAE and was named *Vulture*.

Handley Page O/7 K162/G-EAGN was supplied to China.

Left: Cabin of a Handley Page O/7.

Below: A Handley Page Transport O/10.

Above: A Handley Page Transport O/11.

Below: Handley Page Transport O/10 G-EATK with Bristol Jupiter engines. (Bristol Aeroplane Co.)

Above: The Handley Page W.8.

Left: Cabin of the Handley Page W.8.

Handley Page Transport's W.b *Prince Henry* at Brussels.

Handley Page W.8b
Two 360hp Rolls-Royce Eagle VIII

Span	75ft
Length	60ft 1in
Wing area	1,456 sq.ft
Empty weight	7,700lb
Loaded weight	12,000lb
Maximum speed	104mph
Cruising speed	90mph
Range	500 miles

Handley Page W.8f Hamilton and W.8g

The W.8f was approximately of the same dimensions as the W.8 and W.8b, had accommodation for twelve passengers, but unlike earlier Handley Pages had three engines, unusual in being of two types. The nose engine was a 360hp Rolls-Royce Eagle IX and there were uncowled 240hp Siddeley Pumas mounted between the wings.

One example was built for Imperial Airways and first flown on 20 June 1924, entering service on 3 November 1924. Two more W.8fs were built for Sabena by SABCA. In October 1929, the Imperial Airways aircraft was brought to W.10 standard but with two 480hp Rolls-Royce F.XIIA engines. On 30 October 1930 the W.8g crashed at Neufchatel near Boulogne.

Handley Page W.8f and W.8g

	W.8f	W.8g
	One 360hp Rolls-Royce Eagle IX and two 240hp Siddeley Puma	Two 480hp Rolls-Royce F.XIIA
Span	75ft	75ft
Length	60ft 2in	59ft 4in
Wing area	1,456 sq.ft	1,470 sq.ft

Handley Page W.8f Hamilton G-EBIX *City of Washington* at Cricklewood.

Empty weight	8,600lb	8,100lb
Loaded weight	13,000 lbs	13,780 lb
Maximum speed	103mph	100mph
Cruising speed	85mph	-
Range	500 miles	500 miles

Handley Page W.9a Hampstead

The W.8f had shown the desirability of having three engines of equal power. So the W.9 was produced with three 386hp Armstrong Siddeley Jaguar IV air-cooled radials. It was slightly bigger than the W.8s and had accommodation for fourteen passengers. It first flew on 1 October 1925.

The W.9a went to Imperial Airways as the *City of New York* and, in 1926, had its engines replaced by 420hp Bristol Jupiter VIs. In 1929 the W.9 went to New Guinea as VH-ULK and was destroyed when it crashed into a mountain near Salamua on 31 May 1930.

Handley Page W.9a Hampstead
Three 420hp Bristol Jupiter VI

Span	79ft
Length	60ft 4in
Wing area	1,563 sq.ft
Empty weight	8,364lb
Loaded weight	14,500lb

The three-engined Handley Page W.8f after being modified to W.10 standard as the W.8g but with two Rolls-Royce Eagle engines. (*Flight*)

The Handley Page W.9 Hampstead *City of New York*. (*Flight*)

Maximum speed	114mph
Cruising speed	95mph
Range	400 miles

Handley Page W.10

The W.10 was the last of what can be termed the classical twin-engined Handley Page airliners. Imperial Airways ordered four, insisting on delivery before 31 March 1926. To save time components of the Hyderabad bomber were used combined with the forward fuselage of a W.8.

There was accommodation for fourteen to sixteen passengers, the first aircraft flew on 10 February 1926, the Certificate of Airworthiness was awarded on 5 March and all four were delivered on 13 March.

In a ceremony at Croydon on 30 March Lady Maude Hoare, wife of the Air Minister, named them. They were G-EBMM *City of Melbourne*, G-EBMR *City of Pretoria*, G-EBMS *City of London* and G-EBMT *City of Ottowa*.

The W.10s each powered by two 450hp Napier Lion IIB engines, some from the withdrawn D.H.34s, went into service on European routes. *City of London* was lost in the English Channel on 21 October 1926 and *City of Ottowa* suffered the same fate on 17 June 1929. There were seven fatalities in the second accident. The two surviving W.10s went to National Aviation Day Displays in October 1933 and were used for joy riding. Both were converted to tankers to assist in Sir Alan Cobham's attempted non-stop flight to India. G-EBMM crashed at Aston Clinton, Bucks, on 24 September 1934 and G-EBMR was sold as scrap.

Handley Page W.10
Two 450hp Napier Lion IIB

Span	75ft
Length	59ft 4in
Wing area	1,470 sq.ft
Empty weight	8,100lb
Loaded weight	13,780lb
Cruising speed	100mph
Range	500 miles

Handley Page H.P.42 Hannibal class and H.P.45 Heracles class

In 1928 Imperial Airways invited tenders from the British aircraft manufacturers for a fleet of aircraft to replace older aircraft on the forthcoming Empire routes. Tenders from Handley Page were accepted and orders placed for eight large airliners. Strangely the constructor's numbers given were 42/1 to 42/8 and during their service they were known as H.P.42E (Eastern) and H.P.42W (Western) but post-war research revealed that their true designations were H.P.42 for Empire routes and H.P.45 for Europe. Externally the two types were identical.

These were truly great aeroplanes proving very reliable and with much increased capacity and an outstanding degree of comfort. They were unequal-span biplanes

Handley Page W.10 *City of Ottawa.* (*Flight*)

with fabric-covered metal wings, metal monocoque forward fuselages and fabric covered steel-tube rear fuselages. The wings had Warren-girder bracing and the four Bristol Jupiter engines were mounted two ahead of the upper centre section and two on the lower wing. The lower centre section had anhedral which kept the spars clear of the fuselage and also kept the undercarriage quite short. Passenger accommodation was in two Pullman-like cabins, separated by the galley, mail and baggage holds and lavatories. Normal passenger accommodation was twenty-four in the H.P.42 and thirty-eight in the H.P.45. The cockpit was entirely enclosed.

Hannibal, the first H.P.42, flew on 14 November 1930 following a few earlier hops, and *Heracles*, the first of the H.P.45s, flew on 13 August 1931. The former began operating London-Paris services on 11 June 1931 and *Heracles* followed on 11 September. Both types gave outstanding service with the H.P.45s maintaining European services and the H.P.42s working between Egypt and India and Egypt and Central Africa.

Two H.P.45s, *Hengist* and *Helena*, were modified to become H.P.42s and the H.P.42 *Hanno* was converted to a European aircraft.

On 2 May 1937 *Heracles* made Imperial Airways 40,000th English Channel crossing and on 23 July that year *Heracles* also completed a million miles flying in 10,200 hours, having carried about 80,000 passengers.

Hengist was destroyed by fire in the airship shed at Karachi and, on 1 March 1940, the only fatal accident occurred when *Hannibal* went into the sea between Jask and Shurjah with the loss of four crew and four passengers.

With the Second World War starting in September 1939 the H.P.42s and 45s were operated under the aegis of National Air Communications and several were destroyed on the ground by gales. *Helena* was the last to fly, at Donibristle, near Edinburgh, on a test flight in 1941 after which it was grounded and the fuselage used as an office.

The one disadvantage of these aircraft was their low speed.

Handley Page H.P.42
Four 490hp Bristol Jupiter XI

Span	130ft
Length	92ft 2in
Wing area	2,989 sq.ft
Empty weight	17,740lb
Loaded weight	28,000lb
Maximum speed	120mph
Cruising speed	100mph
Range	500 miles

Handley Page H.P.45
Four 555hp Bristol Jupiter XFBM

Span	130ft
Length	92ft 2in
Wing area	2,989 sq.ft
Empty weight	17,740lb
Loaded weight	29,500lb
Maximum speed	127mph
Cruising speed	100mph
Range	500 miles

Handley Page Type Numbers

Retrospective type numbers allotted to Handley Page civil transport aircraft.

H.P.16	-	O/400
H.P.18	-	W.8 and W.8b
H.P.26	-	W.8f and W.8g
H.P.27	-	W.9a
H.P.30	-	W.10

Saunders-Roe (Saro) A.19 Cloud

From 1930 Saunders-Roe built a series of A.19 Cloud two- and three-engine, amphibian flying-boats. These were high-wing, cantilever monoplanes with Fokker-Avro all-wood wings and metal hulls. They had stabilising floats near mid-span and were powered with various engines which were mounted above the wing.

Seventeen Clouds with Armstrong Siddeley Serval engines were supplied to the Royal Air Force as navigational trainers.

All Clouds were built with single fins and rudders but an Armstrong Siddeley Lynx-powered aircraft was modified to have an auxiliary aerofoil above the engines to reduce landing speed and twin fins and rudders to improve directional control. This twin-fin Cloud was built in 1930 for the Hon. A.E. Guinness and fitted with Pratt & Whitney Wasp engines before delivery. It was sold to Imperial

Handley Page H.P.42 *Hannibal*. (*Flight*)

A corner of the main cabin of an H.P.42.

Handley Page H.P.45 *Horatius* landing at Croydon. (*The Aeroplane*)

Airways in January 1940 for training flying-boat crews and was damaged beyond repair in June 1941.
(Saro Cloud details not shown see T/S page 72.)

Short S.8. Calcutta

The Calcutta three-engine flying-boat was built to operate the trans-Mediterranean section of Imperial Airways forthcoming routes to India and Africa. The hull was a duralumin structure and the wings and tail surfaces were of metal with fabric coverings. The three 540hp Bristol Jupiter XIF engines were mounted side by side between the wings. There was an open two-seat cockpit near the bow and the passenger cabin had seats for fifteen passengers with four rows of three abreast, one row with only two seats and, right aft, a single seat. The cabin measured 17ft in length, 6ft 6in in width and 6ft 3in in height. There were seven windows in the starboard side and six in the port side. The steward's seat, galley and lavatory were at the rear and there was a buffet and oil cooker on the port side.

The first Calcutta was launched at Rochester on 13 February 1928. At the beginning of August, the flying-boat alighted on the Thames and was open to inspection by Members of Parliament at Westminster.

From 24 September to 4 October the second Calcutta operated an experimental Liverpool-Belfast service after which the first and second aircraft operated the Southampton-Guernsey services until the end of February 1929, they were positioned to the Mediterranean where they flew between Genoa or Brindisi and Alexandria.

One of the saloons of an H.P.45.

Saunders-Rose A.19 *Cloud* with auxiliary aerofoil and twin fins and rudders.

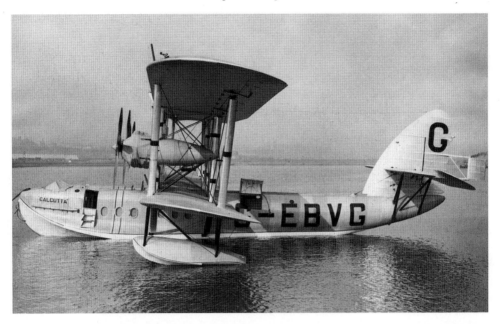

Short S.8 Calcutta *City of Alexandria* on the Medway at Rochester.

Five Calcuttas were built for Imperial Airways and two for France where Breguet built four examples under licence. On the last day of February 1928, Imperial Airways began a weekly service to Central Africa and Calcuttas worked this route from Khartoum to its southern terminal at Mwanza on Lake Victoria. The Calcutta *City of Rome* was forced to alight off Spezia on 26 October 1929 and while being towed it capsized with the loss of three crew and four passengers. The *City of Khartoum* was lost on 31 December 1935 when it ran out of fuel while approaching Alexandria.

After their withdrawal from service two went to Imperial Airways' subsidiary Air Pilots Training for the training of flying-boat crews. G-EBVG, the first Calcutta was re-engined with 840hp Armstrong Siddeley Tiger VI engines in long-chord NACA cowlings. It capsized at Mirabella in 1937 but G-AATZ, also with Air Pilots Training, remained as a crew trainer until scrapped in 1939.

Short S.8. Calcutta
Three 540hp Bristol Jupiter XIF

Span	93ft
Length	66ft 9in
Wing area	1,825 sq.ft
Empty weight	13,845lb
Loaded weight	22,500lb
Maximum speed	118mph
Cruising speed	97mph
Range	650 miles

Short S.8 *Calcutta* after being re-engined with Armstrong Siddeley Tigers. (Short Bros)

Short S.8/8 Rangoon

The Air Ministry issued specification R.18/24 for a flying-boat to equip No.203 Squadron RAF, stationed at Basra. To meet this specification, Short Brothers produced the Rangoon which was virtually identical to the Calcutta except for military equipment and an enclosed cockpit.

The first Rangoon, S1433, was launched and flown on 24 September 1930. Six Rangoons were built and their overseas service ended in August 1935 and the first aircraft was modified in January 1936 as a trainer for Air Pilots Training and registered G-AEIM. It was operated in this form for two years and then scrapped.

Short S.8/8 Rangoon
Three 540hp Bristol Jupiter XIF

Span	93ft
Length	66ft 9½in
Wing area	1,828 sq.ft
Empty weight	14,000lb
Loaded weight	22,500lb
Cruising speed	92mph
Range	650 miles

Short S.17 Kent Scipio class

Due to the closure of Italian seaports to Imperial Airways in October 1929 it became necessary to fly non stop from Mirabella to Alexandria and the airline ordered three flying-boats with sufficient range. These were the Short S.17 Kents.

Short S.8 Rangoon G-EAIM on the Medway at Rochester.

They were named *Scipio*, *Sylvanus* and *Satyrus* and *Scipio* was used as the class name.

The S.17 was generally similar to the Calcutta and had the same form of construction but the cockpit was enclosed and it had four 555hp Bristol Jupiter XFBM engines side by side between the wings. The cabin was 14ft long, 8ft 9in wide and 6ft 6in high, it was furnished to a high standard and had fifteen seats.

Scipio was launched and first flown on 24 February 1931 and the type entered service in May. *Sylvanus* was set on fire and burned out at Brindisi on 9 November 1935 and *Scipio* made a heavy alighting at Mirabella and sank on 22 August 1936. *Satyrus* made a number of route surveys and was finally scrapped in June 1938.

Short S.17 Kent
Four 555hp Bristol Jupiter XFBM

Span	113ft
Length	78ft 5in
Wing area	2,640 sq.ft
Empty weight	20,460lb
Loaded weight	32,000lb
Maximum speed	137mph
Cruising speed	105mph
Range	450 miles

Short L.17 Scylla

In the spring of 1933, Imperial Airways was short of aircraft for its European routes and attempted to buy two more Handley Page H.P.45s but was unable to

Short S.17 Kent *Satyrus*. (Charles E. Brown)

Part of the interior of a Short S.17 Kent.

accept Handley Page's terms and so asked Short Brothers to build two aeroplanes incorporating the Kent flying-boat's wings, tail unit and engines with a new fuselage and land undercarriage.

These two large landplanes were named *Scylla* and *Syrinx* and *Scylla* flew on 26 March 1934, entering service, on the London–Paris route, on 16 May that year.

The new fuselage was a metal-skinned metal structure with a cabin width of nearly 11ft. There was accommodation for thirty-nine passengers in three cabins. At some time *Syrinx* had its two-centre Jupiter engines replaced by Bristol Perseus sleeve-valve engines with ring cowlings and, after overturning in a gale at Brussels, was fitted with Pegasus XC 660hp engines. Its interior was altered to a mock-up for the Empire flying-boats.

In the early days of the Second World War, the two aircraft flew as part of National Air Communications before being requisitioned by the RAF. *Scylla* was blown over at Drem, in East Lothian, Scotland, in September 1940 and *Syrinx* was scrapped in the same year.

Short L.17 Scylla
Four 555 hp Bristol Jupiter XFBM

Span	113ft
Length	83ft 10.5in
Wing area	2,615 sq.ft
Empty weight	22,650lb
Loaded weight	33,500lb
Maximum speed	137mph
Cruising speed	105mph

Short C Class Empire flying-boat

On 20 December 1934, HM Government announced the Empire Air Mail Programme stating that, 'beginning in 1937 all letters despatched from the United Kingdom for delivery along the Empire routes would, so far as practicable, be carried without surcharge'. Imperial Airways estimated that this would involve carrying 2,000 tons of mail a year. This volume of traffic meant that the airline would have to increase its fleet. It was also the airline's view that trunk routes should be operated by flying-boats to eliminate changes of aircraft for different sectors. As a result, Imperial Airways ordered fourteen flying-boats from Short Brothers and soon increased the total to twenty-eight without waiting for a prototype.

The aircraft produced by Shorts was the S.23 Empire flying-boat, which at one time the airline called Imperial flying-boat but all had names beginning with C and the type generally became known as the C class. The S.23 was an all-metal, high-wing monoplane with deep, two-deck hull and four wing-mounted, 920hp Bristol Pegasus XC engines. There was accommodation for sixteen to twenty-four passengers in the main (lower) deck and the crew positions were on the upper deck together with mail holds. Passenger accommodation was divided into several

Short L.17 *Scylla*.

The aft cabin of Short L.17 *Scylla*.

cabins. The front (smoking) cabin had seven seats. Aft of the entrance door, galley and lavatories was the three-passenger midship cabin with seats convertible to bunks, then came the main cabin with eight seats to starboard and a 'promenade' area to port. Right aft was a cabin with six seats.

The Empire boats were unusual because the hulls had no chine; they were flat sided, giving minimum frontal area and maximum internal space. The two 326-gallon. fuel tanks were buried in the wing.

The first S.23, *Canopus*, was launched onto the Medway on 2 July 1936 and made its first flight two days later. The second and fifth boats, *Caledonia* and *Cambria*, had 2,320-gallon fuel capacity and were used on North Atlantic survey flights. The fourth S.23, *Cavalier*, was used on New York–Bermuda services.

On 12 January 1937, Imperial Airways began all-air, trans-Mediterranean services when *Centaurus* left Alexandria for Southampton with a night stop at Brindisi and the first eastbound service left Southampton on 16 January. Empire flying-boats began operating services to Karachi on 3 October 1937. As early as 18 February 1937, *Caledonia* had shown the potential of the long-range type by flying 2,222 miles non stop from Southampton to Alexandria in thirteen hours five minutes and, in July, the same aircraft made the first westbound commercial survey flight across the North Atlantic.

The first stage of the Empire Air Mail Programme was inaugurated on 29 June 1937 when *Centurion* left Southampton with 3,500lb of unsurcharged mail for Sudan, East and South Africa. On 23 February, the Air Mail Programme was inaugurated to Egypt, Palestine, Burma, Ceylon and Malaya and on 28 July 1938, *Calypso* left Southampton with unsurcharged mail for Australia, New Zealand, Tasmania, Fiji, Papua, Norfolk Island, Lord Howe Island, Nauru, Western Samoa and Territories under the jurisdiction of the High Commissioner for Western Pacific.

A number of S.23s were lost in accidents but most passed to BOAC and ten survived until 1947 when they were broken up, and one of the Qantas 'boats', formerly Imperial Airways' *Coriolanus*, was dismantled in 1948. The S.23s were followed by nine S.30s, three of which were operated by Tasman Empire Airways (TEAL). The S.30s had 890hp Bristol Perseus XIIC engines and were strengthened to allow a take off weight of 46,000lb compared with the S.23s of 43,500lb.

On 5 August 1939, Imperial Airways began a weekly experimental service between Southampton, Montreal and New York via Foynes and Botwood using S.30s. The first flight was made by *Caribou* refuelled from tankers working from Shannon and Botwood.

To replace lost aircraft, in 1938 Imperial Airways ordered three S.33 'boats, which allowed a take-off weight of 53,000lb after they had been re-engined with 1,010hp Bristol Pegasus XX1Is. The first two, too late for Imperial Airways, were delivered to BOAC and the third was never completed.

Short C class Empire flying-boats
S.23
Four 920hp Bristol Pegasus XC

Span	114ft
Length	88ft
Wing area	1,500 sq.ft
Empty weight	23,500lb
Loaded weight	40,500lb later 43,500lb
Maximum speed	200mph
Cruising speed	165mph
Range	760 miles

Caledonia and *Cambria* range 3,300 miles.

S.30 Four 890 hp Bristol Perseus XII

Span	114ft
Length	88ft
Wing area	1,500 sq.ft
Empty weight	27,180lb
Loaded weight	48,000lb

Cabot and *Caribou* 53,000lb after in-flight refuelling.

Maximum speed	200mph
Cruising speed	165mph
Range	760 miles

Cabot and *Caribou* range 2,500 miles.

S.33 Four Pegasus XC or 1,010hp Pegasus XXII

Span	114ft
Length	88ft
Wing area	1,500 sq.ft
Empty weight	27,180lb
Loaded weight	53,000lb
Maximum speed	200mph
Cruising speed	165mph
Range	760 miles

Short S.20/S.21 Mayo Composite Aircraft

An aircraft's weight, and thereby range, can be increased if it is refuelled in flight. Similar increases apply if the aircraft is assisted into the air from the back of another aircraft. Major R.H. Mayo of Imperial Airways had worked on the latter solution since 1932 and a contract was placed (with the cost shared by the airline and the Government) with Short Brothers for the construction of such an aircraft.

The lower component, S.21, was generally similar to the Empire flying-boats but had flared chines and an above-the-hull supporting structure to carry the S.20 upper component. The S.20 was a twin-float seaplane powered by four 340hp Napier Rapier V in-line engines and later 370hp Rapier VIs. It

Short S.23 C Class Empire flying-boat *Cavalier* was used on the New York–Bermuda service. (Pan American Airways)

had accommodation for two crew. By air launching, its maximum weight was increased from 15,500lb to 20,500lb.

The lower component, *Maia*, first flew on 27 July 1937 and the upper component, *Mercury*, flew on 5 September 1937. They were flown as a composite on 21 January 1938 and the first separation was on 6 February. *Mercury* made a non stop flight from Foynes to Montreal on 20/21 July covering the 2,930 miles in twenty hours twenty minutes. The flight continued to New York and was the first commercial crossing of the North Atlantic by a heavier-than-air craft.

In October 1938, *Mercury* set a world record for seaplanes. After being launched from *Maia* at Dundee it flew 6,045 miles non-stop to the Orange River in South Africa, with a flight time of forty-two hours and five minutes. *Mercury* was handed over to No.320 (Netherlands) Squadron in June 1940 and *Maia* was destroyed by enemy action in May 1941.

Short S.20 Four 340hp Napier Rapier V
Later 370hp Rapier VI

Span	73ft	
Length	51ft	
Wing area	611 sq.ft	
Empty weight	10,000lb	
Loaded weight	15,500	20,500lb air-launched

The forward, smoking, cabin of a C Class Empire flying-boat.

Imperial Airways Short S.30 C Class Empire flying-boat *Cabot*. (*Flight*)

The Short-Mayo Composite Aircraft.

Maximum speed	207mph
Cruising speed	180mph
Range	3,900 miles

Short S.21
Four 920hp Bristol Pegasus XC

Span	114ft	
Length	84ft 10 ¾in	
Wing area	1,750 sq.ft	
Empty weight	24,000lb	
Loaded weight	38,000lb	27,700lb for air launch
Maximum speed	200mph	
Cruising speed	165mph	
Range	850 miles	

Short S.26 G-class

Imperial Airways required a larger version of the Empire flying-boat for mail or passenger carriage over the North Atlantic. Short Brothers designed the S.26 to meet this requirement and Imperial Airways ordered three.

The S.26 was of the same configuration and construction as the Empire boats, but had modified steps, an enlarged flight deck and an engineer's station. The type was designed to carry five crew and two tons of mail for 2,500 miles against a 40mph head wind. Fuel capacity was 3,600 gallons. Hull depth was 19ft. The first aircraft,

Maia, the S.21 lower component of the Short–Mayo Composite Aircraft at Dundee.

Mercury, the S.20 upper component of the Short–Mayo Composite Aircraft, taking off from the Medway at Rochester. (*Flight*)

Mercury being lowered onto *Maia* on the Tay at Dundee before *Mercury's* record 6,045 miles non-stop flight to the Orange River in South Africa.

Golden Hind, was launched on 17 June 1939 and first flew on 21 July. The second and third boats were to be named *Grenadier* and *Grenville* but this was changed and they became *Golden Fleece* and *Golden Horn*. All three were commandeered by the Royal Air Force and fitted with military equipment. *Golden Fleece* suffered a double engine failure and its hull caved in on alighting in a heavy swell.

On 18 July 1942, *Golden Hind* and *Golden Horn* began working a Poole-Lagos service for priority passengers. *Golden Horn* crashed on a test flight at Lisbon on 9 January 1943 but *Golden Hind* remained in service. None of the boats was ever operated by Imperial Airways although *Golden Hind* was delivered to the airline in May 1939 for training. *Golden Hind* was finally scrapped in May 1954.

Short S.26 G class
Four 1,380hp Bristol Hercules IV

Span	134ft 4in
Length	101ft 4in
Wing area	2,160 sq.ft
Empty weight	37,705lb
Loaded weight	74,500lbs
Maximum speed	209mph
Cruising speed	180mph
Range	3,200 miles

Short S.26 G Class flying-boat *Golden Hind*.

Supermarine Sea Eagle

The Sea Eagle, designed by R.J. Mitchell (later designer of the Spitfire), was a small wooden, biplane, amphibian flying-boat. Three were built and the first was flown in June 1923. It was a two-bay biplane with forward-folding wings, a 360hp Rolls-Royce Eagle IX with pusher airscrew and single fin and rudder. Between the lower wing and the bows was a six-seat cabin, the forward section folding up for loading of goods and baggage. The open cockpit was in the leading edge of the lower wing. The two-step hull, built of mahogany, had a water-rudder at its rear and there were stabilising floats, near the wingtips.

The three Sea Eagles were used to operate British Marine Air Navigation's route from Southampton to Guernsey which opened on 25 September 1923. In service the land undercarriage was removed. One Sea Eagle crashed on 21 May 1924 and is reported never to have been under the control of Imperial Airways, while one was rammed and sunk at St Peter Port, Guernsey, on 10 January 1927. The operation was taken over in 1928 by Short Calcuttas.

Supermarine Sea Eagle
360hp Rolls-Royce Eagle IX
Span   46ft   Span folded 21ft 1in
Length   37ft 4in
Wing area   620 sq.ft

The third Supermarine Sea Eagle at Woolston.

Empty weight	3,950lb
Loaded weight	6,050lb
Maximum speed	93mph
Cruising speed	84mph
Range	230 miles

Supermarine Southampton Mk II

After the loss of Imperial Airways' Short Calcutta *City of Rome* in the Mediterranean in October 1929, the Air Ministry lent a Southampton Mk II to carry mail between Salonica and Alexandria. This was the RAF aircraft S1235, it was allocated the civil registration G-AASH but this was originally wrongly painted as G-AAFH. G-AASH served the airline for three months from November 1929 and was then returned.

The Southampton II was a large equal-span biplane with metal hull and three fins and rudders. It had two 500hp Napier Lion VA engines, the lower wing was strut-braced to the hull and there were wing tip stabilising floats. Another Southampton II was used by the Japanese airline Nippon Kokuyuso Kenkyujo as a passenger aircraft.

Supermarine Southampton II
Two 500hp Napier Lion VA

Span	75ft
Length	49ft 8½in

Supermarine Southampton wrongly painted as G-AAFH. Its RAF service number S1235 appears on the rudder.

Wing area	1,448 sq.ft
Empty weight	9,696lb
Loaded weight	15,200lb
Maximum speed	95mph
Cruising speed	86mph
Range	544 miles

Supermarine Swan

In 1922 Air Ministry placed a contract with Supermarine for a commercial twin-engine, amphibian flying-boat and it was first flown on 25 March 1924. It was an equal-span, two-bay biplane which could have the wings folded forward to save hangar space. The Swan had a two-step wooden hull and triple fins and rudders. The cabin, roughly amidships, had seats for ten passengers, mostly inward facing. A large superstructure on the hull above the lower wing and rear hull contained the open cockpit, was entered by a door in the port side reached by a ladder on the hull.

At first the Swan had two 360hp Rolls-Royce Eagle IX engines but these were replaced by 450hp Napier Lion II Bs. The Swan was awarded its Certificate of Airworthiness on 30 June 1926 and the Air Ministry lent it to Imperial Airways for use on the Southampton-Guernsey route. For this work, the land undercarriage was removed. It was last used during 1927 and was scrapped that autumn.

The Supermarine Swan taking off from Southampton Water. (Supermarine)

The cabin of the Supermarine Swan. R.J. Mitchell, famous designer of Supermarine flying-boats, Schneider seaplanes and the Spitfire is on the right. (Supermarine)

Supermarine Swan
Two 450 hp Napier Lion IIB

Span	68 ft 8in
Length	48ft 6in
Wing area	1,265 sq.ft
Empty weight	9,170lb
Loaded weight	12,832lbs
Maximum speed	108.5mph
Cruising speed	87mph

Vickers Vimy Commercial

In July 1917, Vickers was asked to build a bomber to the same specification as the Handley Page O/400 but with Hispano-Suiza engines. A production order was placed in April 1918 and the type was the Vimy with Rolls-Royce Eagle engines. The Vimy was too late to participate in the war but afterwards the Vimy was used for a number of outstanding flights – the first direct crossing of the North Atlantic and the first flight from the United Kingdom to Australia. Two also took part in the first flight to South Africa.

After the Armistice many orders for military aircraft were cancelled and Vickers turned its attention to the civil market. It was decided to produce a new larger fuselage capable of seating ten passengers, This was the Vimy Commercial and it first flew on 13 April 1919.

In 1919 China ordered forty Vimy Commercials. On 30 April 1920, a Vimy Commercial was delivered to S. Instone & Co.'s Aerial Transport Department. This was named *City of London* and it became one of the best-known British transport aircraft of the period. The fuselage was painted in an attractive royal blue with white lettering. It served Instone until the formation of Imperial Airways and formed part of the new airline's fleet, being withdrawn in 1926.

The Vimy Commercial was of all-wood construction with ply-covered forward fuselage and fabric-covered rear fuselage, wings and tail unit. The engines were two 360hp Rolls-Royce Eagle VIII water-cooled units. They were positioned between the wings and neatly cowled. There was a nose wheel but this was only to prevent the aircraft nosing over.

There appear to have been forty-four Vimy Commercials including the prototype. One was supplied to Grands Express Aériens and one went to the USSR and was used by Dobrolet.

Vickers Vimy Commercial
Two 360hp Rolls-Royce Eagle VIII

Span	68ft
Length	42ft 8in
Wing area	1,330 sq.ft
Empty weight	7,790lb
Loaded weight	12,500lb

Vickers Vimy Commercial G-EASI *City of London* with S. Instone & Co. Aerial Transport Department markings. (Vickers–Armstrongs)

Maximum speed	98mph
Cruising speed	84mph
Range	450 miles

Vickers Vulcan

The Vulcan was an eight-passenger, single-engine biplane of wooden construction. It had single-bay wings, a biplane tail unit and an oval section, unobstructed cabin. The open cockpit was high up, in line with the wing leading edge and reached by a ladder. Instone ordered four Vulcans and the first one flew in April 1922. It was powered by a 360hp Rolls-Royce Eagle VIII and designated Vickers Type 61. It went into service on the London-Paris route; on 1 June 1922 it was followed by two more.

The fourth Vulcan was the Type 63 freighter ordered by the Air Ministry and had an Eagle IX engine. Vulcans Nos 6 and 7 were intended for Qantas but the Vulcan could not cope with Australian temperatures. In fact, Vulcan performance was the subject of legal dispute and two supplied to Imperial Airways as Type 74 were powered by 450hp Napier Lions. These were G-EBFC and G-EBLB, Vulcans Nos 8 and 9. G-EBFC first flew on 3 March 1923 and was withdrawn from service in December 1925 and G-EBLB crashed and burned after take off from Croydon on 13 July 1928.

The cabin of a Vickers Vimy Commercial. (Vickers)

The Air Ministry's Type 63 freighter G-EBEK was exhibited at the 1925 Empire Exhibition at Wembley in Imperial Airways colours but it was never used by the airline.

Vickers Vulcan
Type 61
Rolls-Royce Eagle VIII
Span   49ft
Length   37ft 6in
Wing area   840 sq.ft
Empty weight   3,775lb
Loaded weight   6,150lb
Maximum speed   105mph
Cruising speed   90mph
Range   360 miles

Type 74
Napier Lion
Span   49ft
Length   38ft

Wing area	840 sq.ft
Empty weight	4,400lb
Loaded weight	6,750lb
Maximum speed	112mph
Cruising speed	--
Range	430 miles

Vickers Vanguard

The Vickers Type 62 Vanguard was a twin-engine biplane with accommodation for twenty-three passengers. It was of all-wood construction and was the largest and most advanced commercial landplane of its time. The Air Ministry ordered one and it first flew on 18 July 1923. It was powered by two 468hp Napier Lion engines. Performance was still further improved by replacing the Lions with 650hp Rolls-Royce Condor IIIs. In this form as the Type 103 the Vanguard was delivered on loan to Imperial Airways in May 1928 and redesignated Type 170. It operated on the London-Paris route and then on the London-Brussels-Cologne route. It was returned to Vickers in October 1928 but crashed on a test flight on 16 May 1929.

Vickers Vanguard
Two 650hp Rolls-Royce Condor III

Span	87ft 9in
Length	53ft 10in
Wing area	2,182 sq.ft
Empty weight	12,040lb
Loaded weight	18,500lb
Maximum speed	112 mph

Vickers 212 Vellox

The Vellox was a twin-engine metal biplane with fabric covering. It could accommodate ten passengers, two pilots and a steward but was only used as a freighter. It first flew on 23 January 1934 and it proved to have short take-off and landing runs. Strangely it had no fins but four rudders. There were double cargo doors in the port side. The original engines were two 600hp Bristol Pegasus 1M3s enclosed in ring cowlings and mounted at about mid-gap. Later 600hp Bristol Perseus IIIs were installed. The Vellox was sold to Imperial Airways in May 1936 but crashed and burned after a night take off from Croydon on 10 August the same year.

Vickers 212 Vellox
Two 600hp Bristol Pegasus 1M3

Span	76ft
Length	50ft 6in
Wing area	1,374 sq.ft
Empty weight	8,150lb

Instone Air Line's Vickers Type 61 Vulcan G-EBBL *City of Antwerp.*

Vickers Type 103 Vanguard. (Vickers Aviation Department)

Loaded weight	13,500lb
Maximum speed	157mph
Cruising speed	130mph
Range	690 miles

Vickers Viastra

The Viastra, of all-metal construction with inner and outer fuselage skins of corrugated light alloy, was a high-wing monoplane with biplane tail and two rudders but no fins. There were several versions. The Viastra I (Type 160) with three Armstrong Siddeley Lynx Major, Viastra II (Type 198) two Bristol Jupiter XIF, Viastra III (Type 199) two Armstrong Siddeley Jaguar VIC, Viastra VI (Type 203) one Jupiter IXF, Viastra VIII (Type 230) three Jupiter IFBM, Viastra IX (Type 259) two underslung Jupiter 1XF and Viastra IV (Type 200). Viastra V (Type 202) and Viastra VII (Type 219) were unbuilt projects. The Viastra I first flew on 1 October 1930 and the Viastra X flew in April 1933.

Two Viastra IIs were delivered to West Australian Airways and the Viastra X was built for the use of HRH Prince of Wales. In 1935 it was equipped for testing radio. It was then owned by the Air Minstry and operated from Croydon with Imperial Airways' crews. It was dismantled in 1937.

Vickers Type 212 at Croydon in 1936. (John Stroud)

Vickers Type 259 *Viastra* Mk.X. (*The Aeroplane*)

Vickers Viastra X
Two 650 hp Bristol Pegasus IIL3

Span	70ft
Length	45ft 6in
Wing area	745 sq.ft
Empty weight	7,850lb
Loaded weight	12,350lb
Maximum speed	160mph
Cruising speed	130mph
Range	1,050 miles

Westland Limousine

The Westland Limousine was an attractive two-bay biplane with cabin for three passengers and the open cockpit was above the rear of the cabin on the port side. It was built of wood and made its first flight at the end of July 1919 with the early registration K-126. The engine was a 275hp Rolls-Royce Falcon III. This example became known as the Limousine I and was re-registered G-EAFO.

The Limousine I was followed by six Limousine IIs. The first of these, G-EAJL, had a Falcon engine and the others were fitted with 300hp Hispano-Suiza 42s. The Limousine I and the first Limousine II were lent to Air Post of Banks in autumn 1920 for a short-lived London–Paris service. Two of the other Limousine IIs were used by Instone Air Line from June 1922 and both were scrapped in 1923. Three aircraft went to F.S. Cotton's Aerial Survey Co. in Newfoundland and it is doubtful whether the sixth aircraft was completed.

The prototype Westland Limousine I K-126 with Rolls-Royce Falcon engine. (Rolls- Royce)

The Limousine gained first prize for small class transports in the August 1920 Air Ministry competition. The Limousine I and II were followed by the larger three-bay, six-passenger Limousine III with 450hp Napier Lion II engine. This did not have the attractive lines of the earlier version and only two were built. The first went to Newfoundland and the second, owned by the Air Council, was loaned to Instone Air Line and scrapped in April 1922.

Westland Limousine I
275hp Rolls-Royce Falcon III
Span	38ft 2in
Length	27ft 9in
Wing area	440 sq.ft
Empty weight	2,183lb
Loaded weight	3,383lbs
Maximum speed	100mph
Cruising speed	85mph
Range	290 miles

Westland Limousine II
300hp Hispano-Suiza 42
Span	37ft 9in
Length	27ft 9in
Wing area	440 sq.ft

Empty weight	2,010lb
Loaded weight	3,800lb
Maximum speed	100mph
Cruising speed	90mph
Range	400 miles

Westland Limousine III
450hp Napier Lion II

Span	54ft
Length	33ft 6in
Wing area	726 sq.ft
Empty weight	3,823lb
Loaded weight	5,850lb
Maximum speed	118mph
Cruising speed	90mph
Range	520 miles

Westland IV and Wessex

On 21 February 1929 Westland flew the first Westland IV three-engine, four-passenger, high-wing monoplane. It was of wooden construction, had strut-bracing, three 95hp A.D.C. Cirrus III inline air-cooled engines and wide-track undercarriage. A second Westland IV, G-AAGW, was exhibited at the 1929 Olympia Air Show and this had 105hp Cirrus Hermes I engines.

These two Westland IVs were then fitted with 140hp Armstrong Siddeley Genet Major IA seven-cylinder radial engines and redesignated Wessex. Eight Wessex were produced in addition to the two conversions.

Imperial Airways had G-AAGW as Westland IV, took it back as a Wessex and bought two more and Sabena had four. There was also a strengthened eight-passenger example built for Portsmouth, Southsea & Isle of Wight Aviation.

G-AAGW operated the first railway air service when painted in Great Western Railway colours of chocolate and cream and flown by Captain Gordon Olley. The flight left Cardiff for Haldon and Plymouth in the morning of 11 April 1933 and continued to work twice a day in each direction. The service was extended from Cardiff to Birmingham on 22 May. Then, on 20 August 1934, G-AAGW carried mail from Croydon to Birmingham when the inauguration of Railway Air Services' Glasgow-London Royal Mail service was interrupted by bad weather. On that occasion G-AAGW bore the title 'Railway Air Services' on its nose.

Westland IV and Wessex
IV
Three 105hp Cirrus Hermes 1

Span	57ft 6in
Length	38ft
Wing area	490 sq.ft

Empty weight	3,150lb
Loaded weight	5,500lb
Maximum speed	108mph
Cruising speed	100mph
Range	525 miles

Wessex
Three 140hp Armstrong Siddeley Genet Major IA

Span	57ft 6in
Length	38ft
Wing area	490 sq.ft
Empty weight	3,891lb
Loaded weight	6,300lb
Maximum speed	122mph
Cruising speed	100mph
Range	420 miles

Westland IV G-AAGW at Croydon.

G–AAGW after conversion to Wessex.

Bibliography

Adventurous Empires, Phillip E. Sims, Airlife

Aerial Transport, George Holt Thomas, Hodder & Stoughton

Annals of British and Commonwealth Air Transport 1919-1960, John Stroud, Putnam

Armstrong Whitworth Aircraft Since 1913, Oliver Tapper, Putnam

Avro Aircraft Since 1908, A.J. Jackson, Putnam

Boulton Paul Aircraft Since 1915, Alec Brew, Putnam

Bristol Aircraft Since 1940, C.H. Barnes, Putnam

British Civil Aircraft 1919-1972, three volumes, A.J. Jackson, Putnam

De Havilland Aircraft Since 1904, A.J. Jackson, Putnam

Early Birds, Alfred Instone, Western Mail and Echo

Handley Page Aircraft Since 1907, C.H. Barnes, Putnam

Shorts Aircraft Since 1900, C.H. Barnes, Putnam

Supermarine Aircraft Since 1914, C.F. Andrews and E.B. Morgan, Putnam

The Aeroplanes of the Royal Flying Corps Military Wing, J.M. Bruce, Putnam

Vickers Aircraft Since 1908, C.F. Andrews and E.B. Morgan, Putnam

Westland Aircraft Since 1915, Derek N. James, Putnam

Appendix

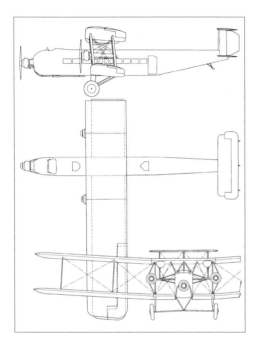

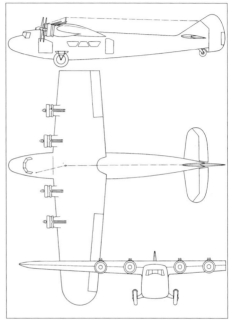

Above left: Armstrong Whitworth Argosy. (Leonard Bridgman)

Above right: Armstrong Whitworth A.W.XV Atalanta. (Leonard Bridgman)

Right: Armstrong Whitworth A.W.27 Ensign. (Leonard Bridgman)

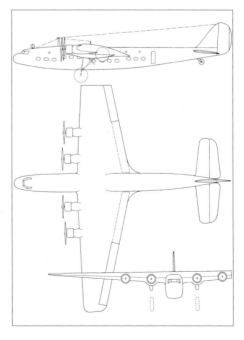

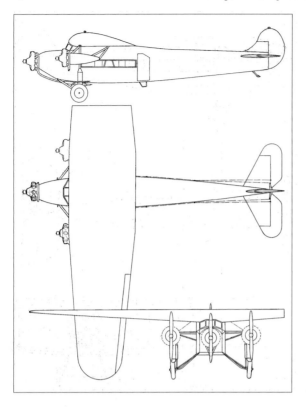

Avro Ten. (Leonard Bridgman)

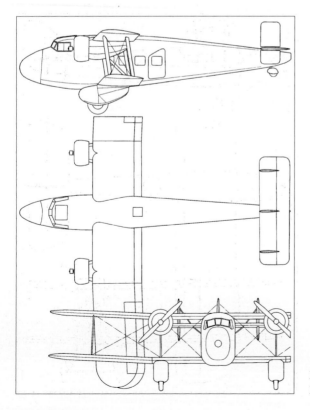

Boulton Paul P.71A *Boadicea*. (Leonard Bridgman)

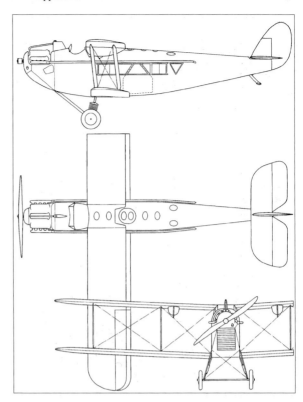

De Havilland D.H.34. (Leonard
Bridgman)

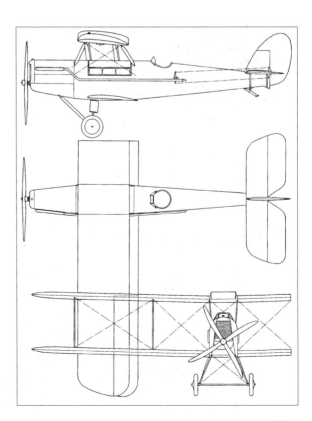

De Havilland D.H.50. (Leonard
Bridgman)

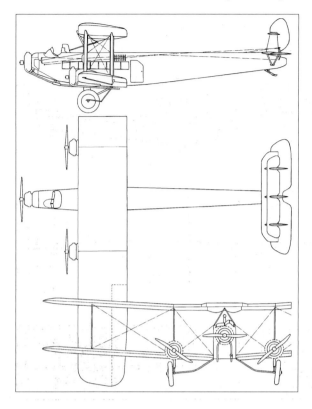

De Havilland D.H.66 *Hercules*.
(Leonard Bridgman)

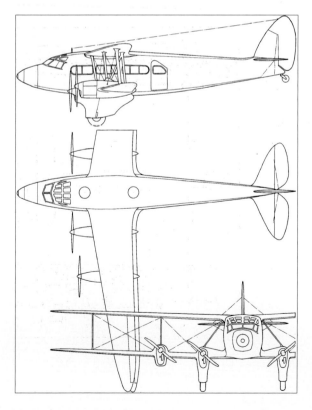

De Havilland D.H.86 *Diana* class.
(Leonard Bridgman)

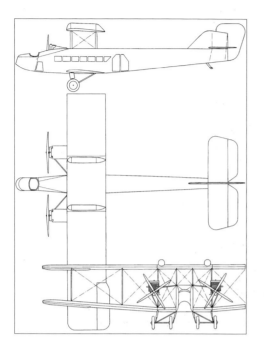

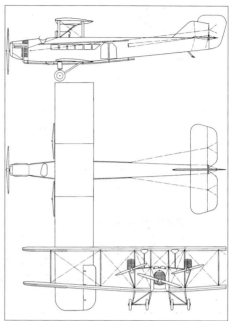

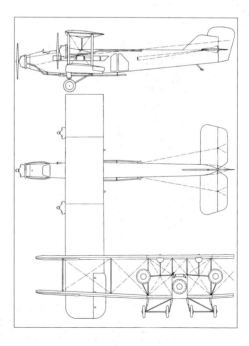

Above left: Handley Page W.8b. (Leonard Bridgman)

Above right: Handley Page W.8f *Hamilton.* (Leonard Bridgman)

Right: Handley Page W.9 *Hampstead.* (Leonard Bridgman)

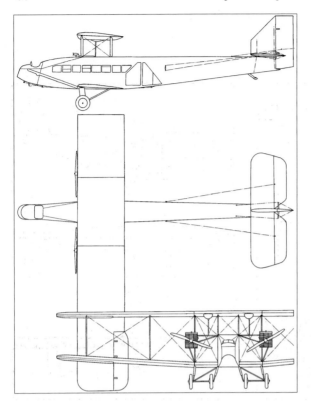

Handley Page W.10. (Leonard Bridgman)

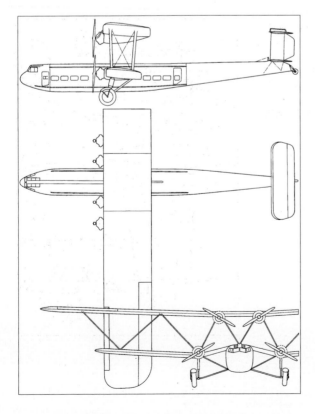

Handley Page H.P.42 *Hannibal* and H.P.45 *Heracles* class. (Leonard Bridgman)

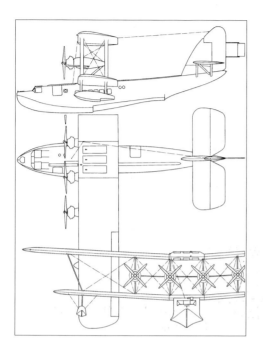

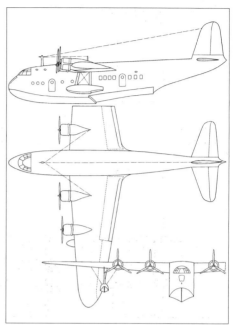

Above left: Short S.17 Kent Scipio class. (Leonard Bridgman)

Above right: Short C Class Empire flying-boat. (Leonard Bridgman)

Right: Short S.20/S.21 Mayo Composite Aircraft. (Leonard Bridgman)

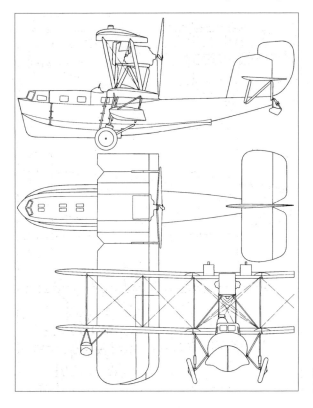

Supermarine Sea Eagle. (Leonard Bridgman)

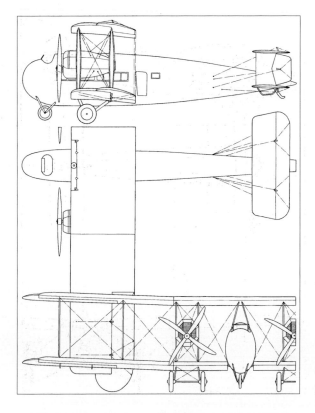

Vickers Vimy Commercial. (Leonard Bridgman)

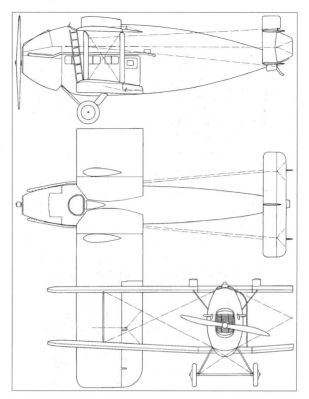

Vickers Vulcan. (Leonard Bridgman)

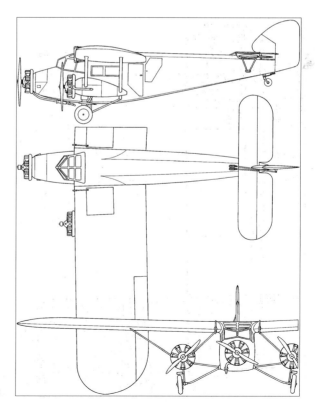

Westland Wessex. (Leonard Bridgman)

Index of Aircraft

Airco
  D.H.4 — 61
  D.H.4A — 61
  D.H.6 — 64
  D.H.9 — 64
  D.H.9A — 64
  D.H.9B — 64
  D.H.10 — 65
  D.H.16 — 66
  D.H.17 — 68
D.H.18 (prototype) — 68
Armstrong Whitworth
  Argosy — 70
  Atalanta (A.W. XV) — 73
  Ensign (A.W.27) — 75
Avro
  Andover (563) — 79
  Ten (618) — 80
  504K — 79
  652 — 80
B.A.T.
FK.26 — 83
Boulton Paul
  P.71A — 85
Bristol
  47 Tourer — 85
  62 Ten–seater — 86
  75 Ten seater — 86
  75A — 86
de Havilland
  D.H.18 (production)
  D.H.32 — 88
  D.H.34 — 88
  D.H.50 — 89
  D.H.50J — 91
  D.H.54 Highclere — 92
  D.H.61 Giant Moth — 93
  D.H.66 Hercules — 95
  D.H.86 (Diana class) — 95
  D.H.91 Abatross — 97

Desoutter
  Desoutter 1 — 99
Handley Page
  H.P.42 Hannibal — 112
  H.P.45 Heracles — 112
  O/7 (H.P.16) — 103
  O/10 (H.P.16) — 103
  O/11 (H.P.16) — 103
  O/400 (H.P.16) — 103
  W.8 (H.P.18) — 104
  W.8b (H.P.18) — 104
  W.8f (H.P.26) Hamilton — 109
  W.8g (H.P.26) — 109
  W.9 (H.P.27) Hampstead — 110
  W.10 (H.P.30) — 112
Saunders-Roe (Saro)
  A.19 Cloud — 114
Short
  S.8. Calcutta — 116
  S.8/8 Rangoon — 119
  L.17 Scylla — 122
  S.17 Kent (Scipio class) — 120
  S.20/21 Mayo Composite — 125
  S.23 C class — 122
  S.26 G class — 128
  S.30 C class — 124
Supermarine
  Sea Eagle — 131
  Southampton II — 132
  Swan — 133
Vickers
  Vimy Commercial — 135
  61 Vulcan — 136
  74 Vulcan — 136
  170 Vanguard — 138
  212 Vellox — 138
  259 Viastra X — 140
  Westland IV — 143
  Limousine — 141
  Wessex — 143

If you are interested in purchasing other books published by Tempus,
or in case you have difficulty finding any Tempus books in your local bookshop,
you can also place orders directly through our website

www.tempus-publishing.com